FINLAND
LIVING DESIGN

FINLAND
LIVING DESIGN
BY ELIZABETH GAYNOR
PHOTOGRAPHS BY KARI HAAVISTO

RIZZOLI
NEW YORK

First published in the United States of America in 1984 by
RIZZOLI INTERNATIONAL PUBLICATIONS, INC.
712 Fifth Avenue, New York, NY 10019

Library of Congress Cataloging in Publication Data

Gaynor, Elizabeth, 1946-
  Finland, living design.

  1. Design—Finland   I. Title.
NK1471.F5G39   1984   745.4'494897   84-42645
ISBN 0-8478-0545-X

Designed by Douglas Turshen

Typeset in New York
Printed and bound in Switzerland

The house is like its master.
—**Finnish proverb**

ACKNOWLEDGMENTS

The author wishes to give special thanks to Walter Anderson, Juliana Balint, Finnair, Finnfacts, Deborah Geltman, Maire Gullichsen, Arto Hallokorpi, Pauli Hatsala, Erik Heinrichs, Kaj Kalin, Ilmari Kostiainen, Barbro Kulvik, Brita Lindberg, Jukka Mäntynen, Terry Martin, Cara McCarty, David McFadden, Bill Meakin, Lynne Creighton-Neall, Tapio Periäinen, Kirsti Rantalainen, Ristomatti Ratia, Maitsu Sihvonen, Kaija and Heikki Siren, Marja Supinen, Tatu Tuohikorpi, Douglas Turshen, Solveig Williams and all those who opened their doors.

CONTENTS

FOREWORD

Finland is one of the world's Meccas of modern design. As a journalist specializing in this field, I made several trips there to report on trends. Members of the design community have come to recognize and expect high quality in furniture, textiles, glass, ceramics, cutlery, crafts, plastics, machinery and even toys from this part of the world over the last thirty years. In the decade following World War II, Finnish designers quietly produced some of the most original, beautifully scaled and well-detailed home furnishings, objects that were fresh but at the same time human. That some special esthetic was operative had been demonstrated in architecture earlier in the century by Eliel Saarinen and Alvar Aalto, two Finns whose reputations on the international scene were by then well established.

By the 1970s so many of the categories in which Finns had pioneered were integrated into contemporary design vocabulary that the impact of their contribution was cushioned by popular acceptance. Graphic cotton fabrics by Marimekko won immediate approval among architects, fashion-conscious women and even students who could afford only a yard of the material to stretch and hang on their walls. Designs for stackable dishes and glasses, and cookware that was handsome enough to move from oven to table, all became kitchen staples by the 1950s. Other recognizable symbols of good Finnish design were now at home anywhere: the orange-handled scissors with a perfect cutting edge, birch and pine furniture, clean modular upholstery, rya rugs. Sauna, a Finnish way of bathing that dates back two thousand years, came to be sought after as much for its physical and psychological benefits as for the thorough cleansing it gives. Another Finnish contribution to American life—the log cabin—was making a comeback as a desirable, country style house.

Trips to Finland reacquainted me with the general excellence of articles that originated there. But the real reward of these forays was the chance to experience the way of living from which the esthetic emerged. A way of sensing—of seeing, touching and perceiving—had as much to do with the fine look and valid function of Finnish architecture and design as had sound logic. Hundreds of years of virtual isolation had taught people to trust their senses, to rely on the work of their hands, to accept and appreciate the ways of nature.

Today Finland enjoys one of the highest standards of living in the world. It was a developing nation that developed in the twentieth century—but did not lose its esteem for traditional values, for the unspoiled environment, for a sense of close community. Two Finnish words come to mind to explain the success of this rite of passage: *Sisu* is a kind of stamina or willingness to stick it out that characterizes both the family that weathers the long arctic night in a carefully constructed log house, as well as the designer patient enough to devise the perfect grip and spout for a coffeepot. *Sointu* means harmony or balance, and typifies the care with which a new house is planned so as not to ruin the natural surroundings, or the restraint with which a piece of fine glassware or furniture is articulated that gives it timeless appeal.

This book is a record through pictures and impressions of a lifestyle, at its best, from which the design sense evolved. It is a glimpse at the unseen Finland, a place that is still largely a forested terrain with country houses tucked in near lakes, down dirt lanes. It is a look into the private homes of a very private people: the renovated turn-of-the-century apartment buildings with simplified Art Nouveau touches, the city houses with inner courtyards or views to the sea, the manor houses of wood with provincial furniture and simply manicured grounds. It gives a taste of sauna, Midsummer, the candlelit dark days of winter—those rituals so characteristically Finnish—and a view of old and new objects for which Finland is celebrated. Here is an attempt to communicate the spirit of living design in a country known for excellence in that area—a place where simple objects are made by sophisticated methods and where a sophisticated architect like Alvar Aalto could explain one of his motifs in the simplest way...from the trim on his mother's bloomers.

LIVING WITH EXTREMES

Swedes we are not, Russians we can never become, so let us be Finns," was a phrase used by one of the early Finnish nationalists to characterize our position in the world. Finland is a country that is both East and West—a country that in the past has been used as a battleground between cultures and ideologies—and that now values its independent life. Privacy is a national preoccupation—we seek it both at home in a city block of flats or in a solitary summer cottage tucked away on an island of its own. Finland is part of the subarctic region that is warmed by the Gulf Stream. This is a land of extreme seasonal variations that greatly influence our way of life. Natural light has a strong esthetic effect on us: there are the nightless nights of summer—the long hours in which day slowly dims into dusk with a delicate play of subtle colors—and the gray and blanketing darkness of winter. Most of all, Finland is a country living very close with nature as reflected in our architecture and design. Ethnologists have not only confirmed this relationship with nature but have gone on to show that it is unlike that of any other European nation. Our attitude is close to that of the Japanese. In the history of our architecture and design this tie takes many different forms: respect for the "soul" of the natural material, placement of buildings in harmony with the environment and inspiration derived from the form's in nature.

Through the ages Finns have built of wood; only our fortresses and churches have been made out of the great lumps of hard granite that is so difficult to work. This means there is very little old domestic architecture left in Finland. Many towns have been destroyed by fire many times over. But because it is a flexible and human material, wood has provided the means for the creation of poetic exteriors and interiors with real feeling, and also for the making of objects that are both functional and esthetically pleasing. In a life dominated by hunting, fishing and farming, the country family historically made all their implements and tools themselves. This way of life held sway until after the Second World War; even in the 1940s about 60 percent of the nation was still country folk. A large proportion of the designers and architects working in Finland today have their roots in this way of life.

When a settler decided to build a permanent home he would first build a sauna as a temporary shelter, then the shed for the animals, the fodder barn and the grain store. Last of all he built his own house. The sauna played a particularly important and profound role as an effective, multi-function building. In addition to its primary purpose as a bath- and wash-house, its heat source was used in many other ways. Today, now that only cleansing and leisure needs have to be filled, designing a sauna's interior and fittings is all the same a true criterion of a Finnish architect's skill. Another traditional element is the *tupa*. It, too, is a multi-purpose room: the living space for cooking, baking, eating, weaving, sewing, tool making and repairs and for sleeping around one major source of heat—the baking oven. The *tupa* traditionally was a true focal point as it still is sometimes in the country-side today.

The old wooden town, in both its winding medieval versions and in the neo-classical rectangular grid plan, was a good place to live: it had low-built wooden houses, a green courtyard behind fence and gate, and out-buildings around the yard. A successful model for town planning in this century is the Käpylä area of Helsinki, designed in the garden-city principle advocated by Ebenezer Howard in the early 1920s. Käpylä incorporates traditional wooden houses, each with its kitchen porch and a small plot for horticulture. Another example is the garden city of Tapiola, west of Helsinki, where up-to-date building construction started in the 1950s. Modern architecture that mixes apartment blocks and family houses along winding streets in a natural woodland setting offers a fine example of our Finnish solution to the integration of urban building and nature.

Alas, not all new construction has been equally imaginative and far-sighted. Thanks to the energetic housing construction programs, and a government housing subsidy in the form of low-interest building loans, the acute housing shortage which grew to explosion point after World War II is just about overcome. But public opinion has sharply criticized many rather monotonous high-rise areas. People have started to demand more one-family houses. Old apartment buildings are also coming back into their own and there has been a great increase in the renovation and modernization of these properties. People have become aware that far too many buildings were destroyed too soon to make way for new ones.

The Finn's passion for nature has demanded a counterbalance to the everyday home: the summer house. It is not such an exaggeration to say that the Finn lives his real life in his country cottage. It is interesting to note that a growing number of rural families, living on farms set amid their own fields, also have a summer or weekend place elsewhere. Here is proof of the Finn's need to detach himself from the concerns of everyday life and a desire to spend time in simpler and more natural conditions far from the pressures of the mechanized world.

In Finland, the long struggle for existence both physically and spiritually has led to the elimination of non-essentials. What is more, frugality is an integral part of our character. But here you will also find richness, vitality and glowing colors to offset the functionality of everyday life and the long dark winter. This dichotomy between plenty and frugality is a source of continuing renewal for Finnish design.

Tapio Periäinen
Director, Finnish Society of Crafts and Design
Helsinki, 1984.

CLASSICS IN CONTEXT

For over four decades, Finnish design has permeated the world of international crafts and industrial production, suggesting that there are some fundamental qualities within the tradition that speak to many people from many places and at many times. In both crafts and in industrial production, Finnish design has been acclaimed internationally by critics, collected by museums and, most importantly, enjoyed by an astonishingly large international audience. Design requires a careful balance between subjective reaction to forms, colors, materials and textures, and the perception of the purpose of the object. It cannot be appreciated or understood on a purely intellectual basis.

The transformation of an object of use into a subject of discussion requires that the personal reaction of the viewer be understood in general terms; my own experience of Finnish design has been guided by the context in which it has been viewed. If I am asked to create a visualization which captures the ambience of Finland, the collage of fleeting images that emerge are the undramatic but pervasive objects and patterns of daily life. I might readily recall the appearance of intense greens, soft grays and subtle browns of a birch forest on the shores of Lake Näsijärvi on a sunny afternoon, or the inviting and comforting table set for a mid-winter dinner among friends in Helsinki, a table furnished with a well-worn and time-bleached wooden bowl, and brilliant glass that transforms candlelight into tabletop fireworks. I might even recall the surprisingly pleasant sensation of a rough linen-weave towel against my skin following a sauna or swim. In all such images, personal and evanescent, the impression and the memory are defined by the context and experienced within the setting in which they exist.

On the other hand, quite a different set of images may be generated from someone who has never traveled to Finland. Beyond the ubiquitous image of the sauna—one universal Finnish stereotype—one may think of the dramatic and imposing glass of Tapio Wirkkala or Timo Sarpaneva, or even the disciplined and harmonious architecture of Alvar Aalto. One might even recall the bright-colored handles on a particularly well-designed pair of Finnish scissors, especially if that user happens to be left-handed. In all of these examples, the perceptions of Finnish design are object-specific; the object carries a message of culture even beyond its native environment. It becomes an interesting paradox why such designs have become a mainstay in the international design movement and yet continue to speak with a Finnish accent.

Our images and sterotypes of the "Finnishness" of Finnish design may have been influenced on two levels: by the carefully conceived and implemented renaissance of design activity within Finland that occurred after World War II, bringing it into the main arena of international competition; and by the ability of Finns to nurture an attitude toward the design process that erodes the artificial barriers between industrial production and the personal response to objects that shape our environment, whether in Helsinki or Hackensack.

Prior to the 1940s, Finnish design was dominated by figures of major significance such as Alvar Aalto and Arttu Brummer who, with others, laid the foundation for modern design that was to be fully appreciated only later in the century. In the 1930s, with the devastating effects of the depression adding to the unavoidable problems of urbanization and rapid industrialization, designers expressed their concerns about the goals of functionalism, the role of industry as a social and cultural force, and the change from a craft-based society to an economically viable manufacturing society. Thought <u>and</u> action were required to maintain the social and aesthetic basis for culture, and the burden of responsibility was clearly laid at the doorstep of the newly emerging industrial designer. The joining of forces—the creativity of the artists and the expertise of industry—was viewed in Finland as the most pertinent and attractive solution to the problems of a modern design-consuming society.

The important experiments of the 1930s, which included the landmark pressed-glass designs of Aino Marsio-Aalto (wife of the architect) for mass production at Karhula Glassworks and the art glass of Gunnel Nyman (whose early death in 1948 cut short one of the most brilliant careers) set the stage for the next phase in the phenomenal progress of Finnish design, which occurred shortly after the end of the Second World War. The determined efforts of organizations such as the Finnish Society of Crafts and Design, which sought to ameliorate the conditions of both industrial designers and studio craftspeople, stimulated innovation within the design community through a determined effort to exhibit the works of designers abroad, and to document the efforts in Finland through major catalogues that accompanied their ambitious exhibition programs of the 1950s and 1960s. It was recognized by critics and by industry that good design could be good business; Finnish industry responded with stepped-up production and quality control and production techniques, but also through the enhancement of the status of the designer within the industry. Rather than producing well-designed but anonymous products, the industries (and particularly those industries that depended upon skilled craftsmanship, such as glassworks) linked the image of the design with the image of the designer. An important transition had been made between indigenous craft and the reality of modern production, and it was this conjoined image of design as production and personality that was disseminated world-wide after mid-century.

The new Finnish spirit of triumph in international design markets was felt as early as 1951, when Finland's contribution to the prestigious Milan Triennale included the work of Tapio Wirkkala, awarded three gold medals for glass design, sculpture and installation of the Finnish section, and Timo Sarpaneva, awarded a silver medal fabric design. Eva Brummer (textiles) and Rut Bryk (ceramics) were each presented with Grand Prix. Also included were Kirsti Ilvessalo (gold medal, textiles), Lisa Johansson-Pape (silver medal, lighting design), Dora Jung (Grand Prix, textiles) and Kyllikki Salmenhaara (silver medal, ceramics). Michael Schilkin, (diplome d'honneur, ceramics) Aune Siimes (ceramics) and Ilmari Tapiovaara (furniture) were likewise accorded honors, the latter two designers receiving gold medals.

This phenomenal success, which brought Finnish design and Finnish designers to the attention of a growing and eager audience of international critics and consumers that emerged after the war years, was followed by even greater triumphs at the 1954 Triennale, when Finnish designers received awards that encompassed a broad range of design from glass and ceramics to furniture and textiles.

The importance of Finnish innovations in form alone cannot be underestimated; the brilliant designs of the late Ulla Procopé for the Arabia factory combined the sleek and sophisticated esthetics of the modern movement with forms and materials that carried with them the timeless quality of the hand-crafted cooking vessel of clay. This kind of brilliance was not a self-conscious striving to deny the industrial process. The glassware designs of Saara Hopea and Kaj Franck, in their genteel simplicity and straightforwardness, reiterated the importance of the esthetic potential of industrial design as manifested in the simplest materials and techniques.

Probably more has been written about the role of materials in Finnish design (and in Nordic design in general) than any other feature of the tradition, a fact that has given a rather unbalanced picture of the real situation. Certainly it is true that the familiarity with a material may bring a sense of confidence to the designer, but if materials were an end in themselves the design tradition of Finland would have much less interest for us than it has. Like the Japanese, Finnish designers seem to be specially able to acknowledge the physical properties of the materials with which they work, and yet transcend both the limitations and demands of the substance. This delicate balance of idea, technique (both craft-based and industrial) and material creates a paradoxical effect to which we readily respond: in Finnish design the combination of dynamic form, unequivocal color and texture and clarity of focus gives the objects a self-assured modesty.

One need only consider the objects of ceramic and glass designer Kaj Franck or textile artist Vuokko Eskolin, or the contemporary ceramics of Minni Lukander to appreciate the delicate balance created between form, material and function that we salute as Finnish. The demands of esthetics are not distinct from the demands of purpose and context in such designs. In retrospect, certain designers who have made significant contributions to our understanding and perception of the Finnish tradition have both reasserted and challenged the role of materials. Probably the most obvious example is to be found in the glass designs of Tapio Wirkkala, whose nature-inspired textures are often combined with an extraordinarily classical recognition of proportion, form and clarity of purpose.

All of the designs that have become "classics" from Finland carry with them a sense of context, thus helping to define the process of design in terms of form and function. This process can be seen as one of the tenets of the new humanism of design that has guided the efforts of the twentieth century, and one in which Finland has played a major role.

David Revere McFadden
Curator of Decorative Arts, Cooper-Hewitt Museum
The Smithsonian Institution's National Museum of Design
New York, 1984

1

INSIDE

PERIOD PIECES

Peasant traditions die hard in a rural people who for centuries have lived in the northernmost outpost of Europe. Like islanders cut off from most of their neighbors by sea, Finns turned inward and became resourceful to survive. Long nights and cold days found people inside carefully constructed squared-log houses in a land where forests cover most of the terrain. While men whittled wood on one side of the room, women worked at spinning and weaving closer to the fire. Separation teaches silence as its natural state. Handwork allows the mind time to wander, to brood on life and its hardships, to dream of tales to explain its secrets.

Outside information reached Finland through Sweden and Russia—countries which brought her Christianity and ruled her by turn for some eight hundred years, beginning in the late twelfth century. Struggles between these two important powers usually involved Finland, sometimes as a battleground, often as a trophy. Cultural influences washed ashore from both West and East and left their mark on the lifestyle and crafts of the people. By the seventeenth century, the grandest houses belonged to a landed gentry appointed to administrate and protect the duchy by the Swedish king. But by standards elsewhere in Scandinavia and Europe, these manor houses were simple—most were boxy wooden homes whose log construction had simply been covered over by smoothed clapboard that could be painted and trimmed for decoration.

Hard work and tenacity were key to Finland's survival in a harsh climate and under outside rule. Self-sufficiency paid off. The grand duchy was more prosperous by the late nineteenth century and felt herself ready to move away from the Imperial Russian regime that had dominated her for nearly a hundred years. Finland fell in love with her own past and in a true cultural revolution, her rebellion against foreign domination first took artistic form. This was a golden age for arts and design. Local artists went off into the forested wilderness, as Gauguin went to Tahiti and Van Gogh to the south of France, to be inspired by nature and man in a more primitive habitat. Within their own borders, however, Finns did not have far to go. Motifs from stark medieval churches and chimneyless log huts, still then in use, served as fresh inspiration for the most interesting new decorative objects and houses. It was the time of romanticism on a national scale. Jean Sibelius celebrated the glorious native culture in music. Poets and painters interpreted scenes from epic folk tales or family life in the woods. Imagine the surprise at the Paris World's Fair of 1900 when architects and artists from this small backwoods province produced the most original pavilion of the exhibition: it was the sensation of the show among worldly Europeans.

In the 1930s and 1950s such surprises were repeated, this time in world design fairs in both Stockholm and Milan. Contributions by Finns, by now representative of an independent nation, again were show-stoppers and won highest honors in competition. Cognizant of the new technologies of the day, Finnish architects and designers were working in the functionalist mode, their brand of the international modern style. But as in Paris at the turn of the century, they looked to what they knew best for inspiration—the marriage of plain shapes and honest materials, forms that derived from the simple splendor of Finland's past. Their entries were not derivative. The stands and their contents were streamlined and innovative, a fresh harmony of artist-conceived industrial design.

Three main styles emerge as we look at how Finns live today and think about their history. Here, the terms country, romantic and modern are used to interpret these influences which have their origins in Finland's design heritage, but without the intention of limiting them to only certain periods. Thus, country style houses qualify as both the well-preserved old log houses and those homes built or furnished today in that deliberately simple look. Stylistically, romantic expression in Finland takes many forms, but it is never very fussy. More than one particular look, it is a way of consciously looking back into the past and bringing forward in time selective elements from nature or primitive decorative detail, or from the exotic creations of Finland's neighbors to the east and west. It shows in a spirit of living and a way of reviving bits of the old, of setting a mood that is both emotional in tone and artistic in character. Modern is the look with which Finland has come to be so closely associated in the post-World War II era. Houses and apartments of the style are open and intentionally uncluttered, airy and light, but somehow always human in scale and natural in feeling. As elsewhere today, sometimes they are furnished with only industrially produced things of our era, but more often tend to mix in some craft or a few well-chosen antiques.

Following are three houses that are now thought of as landmarks of the periods in which they were built. Each characterizes its time, but is atypical in the sense that it embodies some of the best design and craftwork then available. The first is the farm home of an eighteenth-century gentlewoman. While most people then (and indeed well into the next century) were living in simpler log dwellings, Frugård is representative of a fine country house of its time. Secondly, Hvitträsk is the remarkable studio house of Eliel Saarinen, Armas Lindgren and Herman Gesellius, a partnership of the young, most promising architects of their day. It incorporates outstanding decorative detail and crafts in a setting of fine architecture and epitomizes the idealistically artful approach to life in the first decade of this century, Finland's National Romantic period. The most recent of the three examples is Alvar Aalto's Villa Mairea, his residential masterpiece in the functionalist style of the late thirties that typifies his intuitive approach to the modern idiom.

The romantic mood of turn-of-the-century Finland is captured by this reproduction from the pages of *Ateneum* magazine in 1901. The watercolor of a sitting room is one of a series of *Villa Fantasies* by Eliel Saarinen.

FRUGÅRD: 18TH-CENTURY COUNTRY STYLE MANOR HOUSE

The manor house, as seen from the rear and front, is flanked by several outbuildings. The single-tone painting of the seesaw-type bench, fence and house gives it a naive charm.

Finnish manor houses possess a charm all their own. Unlike the castles of southern Europe and distinct from estates in neighboring Nordic countries, these were provincial homes in a frontier region that had no royal lineage or privileged nobility. This was the territory settled since before the time of Christ by migrants from the Volga and east Baltic regions, and long inhabited by the Lapp tribes of the north—the wilderness conquered by Sweden during the Crusades. Stylish country dwellings were first built on landgrants given Swedes dispatched to the outpost by their king. The properties remained in families or were later purchased by educated and merchant classes. The earliest manor houses range in style from those few of several stories in stone or stucco to the glorified farmhouses in wood found in the more remote areas.

Frugård is of the latter type, built on farmland in 1790 by Mrs. Hedvig Juliana Munck, who had come to own the property some years earlier. She enlarged the existing working farm and gave it its name, which means Madame's Estate. The house is homey and comfortable, an expression of fine bourgeois taste rather than a formal or overly grand monument to the then current court-favored classical style. Except for the front vestibule and kitchen porch added later, the main house and outbuildings are preserved just as they were. Of log construction with corner posts, the house has a veneer of vertical planks painted ochre for added protection against the

Long views are offered by an allée of birch trees along the main drive and by the interconnected interior spaces, each room hand-painted with a different motif. White linen runners are tacked down at either end.

weather and a fancier appearance. Its elongated form is the logical extension of the basic one-room house from which the larger farmhouses derive. In the countryside, families added to their homes as time and resources allowed, often starting with one cabin and attaching similar self-contained rooms side by side. It is a sign of the prosperity of this farm that the house was conceived as a multi-roomed whole with attic and tiled mansard roof. An open-ended courtyard is formed out front, in the customary way, by positioning major outbuildings so they flank the main building, with other barns, stables, haylofts and such scattered more freely at some distance. The manor is remarkable outside as in for the balance and consistency of its style, a well-kept souvenir of the late eighteenth century, known in Sweden/Finland as the Gustavian period.

Swedish King Gustav III had taken the throne by coup in 1772, but as proof of his wish to rule as an enlightened despot he expressed great interest in cultural concerns and in particular in the refined styles of the model democracy of ancient Greece. He introduced neo-classical forms into the architecture of Sweden, and especially into interiors by reinterpreting the classical influence on French and English court styles of the day. Frugård with its symmetrical layout, decorated walls, painted wood furniture and overall pale palette is one of the finest intact

examples of Gustavian influence on a Finnish interior of that period. The log walls of all the main rooms were covered with linen and painted in oils by an artist who might have been commissioned from Stockholm where Mrs. Munck's son was chief stable master to the king. The *faux* painted effect of panels and pilasters was a relatively inexpensive way to give the square rooms an elegant architectural feeling. Figurative motifs range from hunt still-life scenes to floral bouquets to swags, organized amongst a repetition of naive columns, each theme assigned to one room.

The delicate use of color and the quantity of freestanding furniture were further evidence of the owner's means and taste. Important pieces were imported—mostly from Stockholm and perhaps even one from France—others were homemade by itinerant carpenters or full-time farm hands. Pewter, the poor man's silver, is the dominant metal for accessories like candlesticks and bowls. Others are of brass or gold leaf over wood, a way to give ormolu-like sparkle to clocks and mirror frames at lesser expense. The burnished golden tones over gray of the wall painting subtlely tie together the mix of metals. Seating areas are arranged characteristically with a bench and suite of matched chairs around a table lightly draped with linen or crochet. Occasional tables, chests and extra chairs stand along the perimeter of the room. Of special note are some of the built-in pieces. Even the large corner heating stoves, which, by the middle of the eighteenth century were made of tile, show classical influence in their form. An unexpected mini-gallery of turned wooden legs lifts and lightens their mass and buffers the floor against stray sparks. An unusual large closet was built on one side of the main living room for practical storage purposes in such a way as to balance the bulk of a stove that sits in the opposite corner. Its painted-out color and applied moldings indicate the desire to tie it in to the architecture of the space.

Frugård is a mannered country lady of a house, possessing an unforced, comfortable dignity. The imagination of its first owner shows in her ability to make a working farm also a gracious home for musical evenings and parties by giving to the rather simple rural surroundings a taste of the worldly pleasures of the time. Later generations of the family have added their own touch as the house came to be theirs, all the while respecting its integrity and caring for its special contents.

The elegant wall painting in this sitting room is considered to be stylistically the purest example of such Gustavian work in Finland. The furniture is of the period and shows influence of both Louis XVI and Queen Anne styles. The clock was made in Stockholm in the mid-1800s and the bombé chest is thought to be from France. A pewter collection includes snuff boxes and candle-wick scissors.

A pine floor painted butterscotch, its original color, warms pale walls in the sitting room and enhances a tiled stove and *ryijy* rug woven at the farm.

In the main living room are Gustavian straight-back chairs, and splat-back, cabriole-leg Queen Anne type chairs, with 19th-century family portraits by Lindt hanging above. Nearby stands a strikingly simple interpretation of a French commode and an unusual built-in closet.

The vines-and-ribbons theme of a side room is seen through a door frame with hunt motif painted above an arbor-like vine. Painted walls are used spatially: artwork, mirrors and clock are centered in the *faux* panels.

HVITTRÄSK: A UNIQUE STUDIO HOUSE

Seldom do architects get the opportunity to design not just a house but create the whole of its interior from trim to furnishings. At Hvitträsk a rare trio of young talent was motivated by the sweet taste of first success: theirs had been the much-praised design for the Finnish pavilion at the Paris World's Fair in 1900. Here was the chance to act out their beliefs more lastingly in a new kind of inside/outside architecture based on truth to materials, appreciation of simple volumes and respect for use. These were radical ideas in an age of revivalist thinking that produced great demand for banks that looked like Gothic churches, houses that copied Italian palaces and apartments

that resembled temples of ancient antiquity in all the major world capitals. The three architects, Herman Gesellius, Armas Lindgren and Eliel Saarinen, bought a parcel of land in the woods and started plans for a studio house for themselves—a sort of artists' paradise, experimental structure, communal living set-up, and soon-to-be salon for all the great creators of their acquaintance.

The firm Gesellius, Lindgren & Saarinen was established in 1896 before the group had graduated from architecture school. Their union represented a balanced meeting of the minds and pool of skills. Lindgren was the scholar, Gesellius the pragmatist and Saarinen the artist, with a painter's training and eye. Together, they produced a compound situated on a bluff high above Hvitträsk (White Lake) and took its name for their dwelling. Homes for the three and their wives were built, one freestanding, the other two joined by a single-story studio with skylights. The architects played up the spectacular setting with a textural structure that seemed to grow up out of its rock foundation set on the wooded cliff with natural outcroppings. Further, a system of outdoor terraces, pavilions and porches were executed to set off

the lovely open view with fretwork and dark shingles, red tiles and climbing vines that change to a hue in autumn like that of the trim.

Work began on the project in 1902. The first building to be completed was a workshop and stables, later to become the home of Gesellius. Its dark-stained timber construction and that of the partly plastered-over stony main building showed the admiration of the three for strong deliberate forms and simple materials found in nature, and used in the log houses of Finland's eastern wilderness province of Karelia and in the high-peaked medieval churches that strikingly accented the horizon. But more than that, looking back to those primitive structures was part of the rebirth of relating building shape to interior space, part of a new way of thinking that was to make use of the latest construction techniques to create a house with open rooms that flowed into one another and use interior fittings that were integral, not just applied. The three designers paved the way toward modern through the National Romantic: it was in looking back and romanticizing the simpler past that the team was to progress in their work beyond the then popular facade-heavy building styles.

The design for the studio house incorporates the natural surroundings. Stone walls tie-in to a rock foundation; both rise from the ridge high above the lake. The architects built from materials at hand—timbers from the forest, granite from the slope. Views in all directions are provided by high gables, towers and balconies; around the grounds, walkways, terraces and overlooks lead one toward the panorama. The idyllic setting was conducive for work and suggestive of motifs for the firm's projects. As Saarinen put it, "One must go down to the source of all things: to nature."

The integration of inside and outside was abetted by their desire to design the interiors and furniture, and to invite some of the great artists and craftsmen of their day to contribute to the work. Like the Continental architects working in the Arts and Crafts style of William Morris, they believed the way to beautify a house was by use of the handmade. Saarinen designed most of the furniture in the rooms here, the wing that he and his wife Loja lived in with their family for nearly twenty years. In 1923 they left for Chicago after he had won second prize in the prestigious Tribune Tower competition; the architecture firm had broken up and the others had moved some years earlier. Loja collaborated on the interiors and was herself a skilled weaver. She made the *ryijy* (rya) rugs that swept over built-in banquettes and down onto the floor. Glazed tiles for the fireplaces and stoves in all the rooms were

This room was artfully painted by Akseli Gallen-Kallela, a multi-talented man who embodied the ideal arts and craftsman of his day. The furniture and lighting were designed by Eliel Saarinen and the *ryijy* rug by Loja Saarinen. A telling stained-glass triptych depicts the young Saarinen at left, Gesellius at right and Mathilde, the first Mrs. Saarinen, pondering in the center. She later left her husband for Gesellius, whose sister Loja married Saarinen.

made at the Iris factory of Count Louis Sparre in Porvoo, known for its excellent handwork. Celebrated fine-arts painter, Akseli Gallen-Kallela, did the frescoes in a dramatically vaulted room. Color was used generously to give a rich completeness to each room and create harmony with its adjacent space. A great imaginative spirit and flair for the exotic show in interpretive furnishings and precision of detail.

The great hall at Hvitträsk echoed the spirit of Karelia in deep color and use of exposed timbers. At its core is a grand tile fireplace with its gleaming cylindrical shape, graceful copper hood and cast-iron rings on a corner post grasped for balance by late-night orators at the Saarinens' parties.

The house seems to have fulfilled the dream of its designers. Its studio gave birth to a list of important architecture built by the group and, after their firm split up, by Saarinen alone. Its large halls and intimate nooks, gardens and walkways, served as enriching atmosphere for the Saarinen children who spent their childhoods here and as lively entertaining space. A wide circle of friends that included Jean and Aino Sibelius, Maxim Gorky, Gustav Mahler among other sculptors, writers, painters and architects were notorious for their all-night celebrations sometimes playfully recorded in the sketchbooks of Eliel Saarinen.

The architects' well-lit atelier has a vaulted fireplace framed by built-in banquettes. At far left, is the nursery, now refitted with a double bed, and above it, the study for the allegorical stained-glass triptych. White furniture and woodwork for the master bath, bedroom dressing area and adjoining sunroom are reminiscent of furnishings by Arts and Crafts designers working concurrently on the Continent.

VILLA MAIREA: A MODERN LANDMARK

One of the great artistic paradoxes is that through the expression of his own uniqueness, a creator often speaks most clearly to the community of man. Not only was the young architect Alvar Aalto able to do both in his lifetime, but such was his intention early on. Even for the building of a single luxury house, his writings on the project clearly indicate his interest in social issues as part of his work, in finding models for universally applicable solutions. The house commissioned in 1937 by industrialist Harry Gullichsen and his wife Maire was to be for all those concerned, including Aalto's architect-wife Aino, an experiment in forms, materials and techniques which would suit the specific needs of a growing family, but which would also yield models for housing and public building in Aalto's future work.

By this time, Aalto had won architectural competitions and both national and international acclaim for two of his breakthrough projects in the emerging modern style—the Viipuri Library and the Paimio Sanatorium. Harry and Maire Gullichsen, as cultured and far-sighted as they were socially idealistic, understood and admired Aalto's work. In the next few years they were to form a kind of personal and professional partnership with him that was to last until his death in 1976. Maire Gullichsen, a painter and art collector, founded, with the Aaltos and another colleague, an interior design and art gallery to create interiors for its clientele and sell affordable furnishings of the Aaltos' design. The company was called Artek, a name which stood for their shared belief in the potential happy marriage between art and technology in the twentieth century. Simultaneously, Harry Gullichsen offered Aalto the opportunity to design an important pulp mill and its worker housing for Ahlström, the large company he headed. Villa Mairea was commissioned as a result of success in both undertakings.

"Aalto felt a house should be like a harp," says Maire Gullichsen, "with outside walls but open on the inside." Villa Mairea's very fluid and inviting interior space stands open on its ground floor, save the kitchen and Harry Gullichsen's study enclosed by light wood walls that appear to float. Natural materials were selected for use both inside and out as a way of tying the house to its surroundings and of interpreting new functionalist principles, that justified design by its usefulness, in a warm and humanistic manner. It was Aalto who, after the architecturally conservative 1920s in Finland, had picked up the lead of Saarinen and Lindgren (at one time his teacher) and pushed forward with their theories in surprising new ways. At the same time he incorporated some of the tenets of the Bauhaus which called for cohesive environments of industrially produced elements. With new technology and his creativity, Mairea was a testing ground for these modern goals: forms could be more than ever allied to function; freer exterior shapes could speak of new interior use; nature could serve as a design model and also play a

Villa Mairea's form and surface are at once functional, romantic and playful. The exterior reads as an experiment in wood techniques and as an intriguing, artful whole. White plastered surfaces, inside and out, are humanized with horizontal and vertical wood slat or pole treatments, windows that punch out at an angle, and an organic tower shape that brings light to a painting studio.

daily role in the life of the home, brought closer through large expanses of glass; elegant furnishings could be serially produced to complement contemporary interiors.

Aalto observed themes in nature and reinterpreted them for Villa Mairea. The rhythms of the nearby forest were repeated in posts used to support canopies linking entry and courtyard to the body of the house, and

The courtyard lawn includes a turf-roofed sauna and swimming pool shaped something like an Aalto glass vase. The sauna's wrapped posts carry the motif along, and its slatted benches and stove are treated with ascetic elegance. Nearby, Aalto's primitive gate grows out of the terrain to link up with a rough stone wall, in harmony with the simple spirit of sauna.

again in the interior posts of the hallway and main stairs. The exposed steel columns that carry the 250 square meters of open living space were staggered idiosyncratically and wrapped with caning or wood to echo their all-wood counterparts outside. Native clay, stone and brick were used inside as well as out. Natural tones and neutral colors were specified because Aalto felt them to be beautiful in their own right and because they were to serve as a clean background for a good collection of modern art.

The systems of the house are as functional as they are handsome. A series of compartments in the library walls are made to hold canvases so paintings could be rotated as the collection grew. The Finnish pine ceiling is

slotted with some 52,000 pin holes in the spaces between slats to provide unobtrusive ventilation and heating. Sculptural plaster and stone fireplaces, different in each room, supplement the heat. Most of the furnishings and lighting was designed by Aino Aalto with her husband to be simple but sub-

Natural materials are treated sensuously. The stone and plaster fireplace, with its signature curve worked gracefully into the profile view, forms a focal point for the main seating area. A medley of wood posts leads from entry to open living space. The study is formed by a wall that is pierced near the ceiling and backs up to a Danish piano designed by Paul Henningsen in 1930.

stantial enough for the open spaces and to keep a low profile, giving the rooms a feeling of airiness. The building looks toward an expansive front lawn and turns back on a grassy courtyard with a swimming pool, formed loosely by the shape of the house, veranda and sauna. Over the years, nature has grown up to embrace the undulating structure in a warm and fitting way. In Villa Mairea, Aalto achieved not only the bridge he sought between man and nature, but a harmony between man and manmade that was to have lasting impact on architecture and design in Finland and throughout the world.

Detailing in both open areas and private rooms remains consistent and naturalistic. Here are shown a corner seating area in the living room, and the fireplace with its console-like granite hearth in the dining room. The kitchen's partly open storage shows off a collection of copper pots and Maire Gullichsen's own opal glass designs. Upstairs is her painting studio and the playspace of the children's wing.

COUNTRY ROOTS

Finland is a land with its heart in the country. The Finnish soul is at home in a grove of birches, picking the first wild mushrooms of autumn, scrubbing a rag rug on a smoothed rock by the sea, or weaving at a loom on a winter evening. One senses a rustic presence in even the most up-to-date houses, where the open-plan living, centered fireplace and warm sauna echo country roots.

Such home features are not uncommon, but rather are as old as some of the oldest Finnish dwellings. The earliest log houses were open one-room structures. (This is the same style of log cabin that influenced Americans in the 1600s when the first Finns emigrated to the state of Delaware.) Inside, massive stone stoves were used for both cooking and heating. People sometimes also bedded down for the night on mattresses laid in the cozy space atop their radiant surfaces, in a loft-like arrangement, or spread straw pallets on the warmed floor nearby. The multi-purpose room, or *tupa*, served for living/working/eating and saw much use especially in the dark winter months when outdoor pursuits were largely curtailed.

Plain built-in furniture—benches and long pine table for dining, cupboards for storage—unwittingly anticipated much later demand for easy care, streamlined furnishings. The sauna was a necessity and was often built as a freestanding unit before the house. The family could live there as the construction of the main building proceeded, cook for the time being on its primitive rock fireplace, and bathe within in the custom of the times.

In Finland, country is an attitude and, indeed, a way of life. Not restricted to the vicarious enjoyment of collecting antiques, folk art or handmade provincial pieces, country living for most Finns is a routine part of their weekend and summertime pleasure, if not a fulltime involvement. Rustic weekend houses dot coastline and lakeside, others lie deep in the forest...all as intentionally unobtrusive as a seagull at roost or an elk asleep by a mossy rock. Long a land of farmers, hunters and fishermen, Finland remained virtually an agrarian culture until after World War II, making its international success in modern design during those years all the more startling. Today, country customs endure in both town and rural areas simply as part of the fabric of time-tested and traditional life, as evidence of the way people behaved in the not-so-distant past.

Sensible solutions to the problems of living, honed by extremes of climate and geographical isolation, were passed along naturally from rural relatives to contemporary cousins. Many houses today are designed in the country style. Peaked boxy shapes remind one of the continued importance of layout and good heating in this northern land. Effective insulation is a matter to be taken seriously and still is partially accomplished in homes of older construction by massive logs notched and joined tight like fine cabinetry. Openings are limited in surface with multiple windows and closings that allow insulating dead air space between. Roofs are pitched against overloads of snow. Effectively, Finns are years ahead of many of us in the northern hemisphere in the construction of energy-aware houses and apartments, whose primary operating principles derive from backwoods wisdom.

In looks, an easy and unselfconscious harmony is the legacy of Finland's country roots. Wooden houses still predominate in the countryside and even in those neighborhoods of towns fortunate enough to be undisturbed by fires that took their tolls in the last century. Red and ochre are everywhere traditional colors for painting wooden houses. As earth colors, they were easy to come by starting about 150 years ago—the recipe for mixing up a home brew consisted of earth, eggs, oil and oatmeal—and cosmetically, they imitated the finer materials of brick and limestone. Their white-trimmed doors and windows cleanly punctuate colorful slatted facades.

Naturals—like wood, wool, cotton and linen—decorate most country style houses. Pine or birch furniture (painted pieces usually originating in the western Swedish-speaking region), bowls, cookware and baskets, and scrubbed pine floors (not "pickled" in the English or American way, but literally washed down periodically as part of the cleaning process) dominate the interior landscape. Cotton curtains and furniture covers with tightly woven stripes or naive checks and windowpane plaids, multi-hued rag rugs (many still homemade) striping stairways and floor boards, and puffy feather comforters—all soften the lines of wood. Woolly small-patterned *ryijy* rugs or sheepskins are used almost anywhere warmth is desired—on furniture or floors, or even hung on walls. Everywhere a sense of tidy usefulness recalls the simpler past. Country people made no distinction between crafts and design; interiors were all of a piece and everything worked. A taste for no-waste developed in this rural people and finds expression in sturdy furnishings fashioned with precision. That so many are still in use today attests to the country craftsmanship that went into their making.

Decorative surprises are the delicately ornamented trundle beds that date from the 1700s and that proved their worth historically in multi-purpose room plans, the squat carved-back wedding chairs with their geometric motifs carefully made and offered by a groom to his eighteenth- or nineteenth-century bride. And there are the ceramic stoves, some in solid colors, some with patterns in relief or glaze, that replaced their early bulky stone counterparts and still today stand handsomely but unobtrusively in the corners of rooms, quietly giving back twelve hours of heat for every hour of fire fueled in their bellies. Today, the country look can be found in small villages and city apartments alike. The Finns, like others of us, are rediscovering and celebrating their more primitive past, and are preserving the wooden houses that now contrast so interestingly in the contemporary milieu.

THE SIMPLE RICHNESS OF A KARELIAN LOG HOUSE

Just as this log house stands at the edge of the forest, so it might have nestled in its original setting in the heart of the province of Karelia. Log by log it was rebuilt near the south coast by Armi Ratia, best known as the creator of Marimekko, who managed to have it moved when that territory was lost to the Russians in 1945. Every beam of the seventeenth-century house was well-known to her since it had been the home of her grandfather. Today the bittersweetness of its history is matched by its chocolate box mix of furnishings which range in tone from mocha to deepest brown. Some are old things that belonged to the house, others are characteristic of the region and period. Finds from other parts of Finland add depth to the woody blend.

Used for sleeping and sitting, this room was built as an addition to the original one-room house. In this region where people were of the Orthodox faith, a visitor first faced the icon to pay his respect before greeting the host.

Built in characteristic rectangular shape, the house first consisted of the main room only where activity centered around the generous hearth. Here handwork was done on the loom or lap, wide-banded embroideries and weavings in the Eastern-influenced Karelian style. In respect to tradition, all the homespun curtains suspended simply on string at each window and long rag runners that stripe the rooms were woven more recently on the loom that is original to the house. On closer inspection the *tupa* has all the ingredients for daily family life. Against the wall closest to the stove, are the wooden kitchen things: cutting boards, butter box, square molds with carved geometric surfaces to decorate cured cheeses, root whisks, well-hollowed-out spoons (for a long time the only eat-

Typically, the log houses of Karelia were not painted or stained outside or in. Textiles were the chief source of color against deep wood tones. Today the simple rooms are more fully dressed than when they were new. The main room was built in 1609; it housed several people and served all living purposes. It was always generous enough in scale for working, even for building a sled or a piece of furniture during the cold winter months. The oven was used for both heating and cooking, and was important for baking in this area known for its hearty grain breads and stewpot meals.

48

ing implement) and that wonderful multi-purpose utensil, ingenious in its simplicity—a stick carved in one piece from a crotch of young pine bearing several branches, that in the kitchen is used to blend porridge or other batter. One rolls its upright stem between two hands which whirls its spiky branches in beater fashion. Across the room stand the familiar long pine table and benches—those that are built-in around the perimeter of the room could serve as extra sleeping places—a short rocker with sheepskin throw, a hutch and the loom. Tucked up high like a nest on the flat of the stove is the straw mattress and bedding of the main sleeping area.

Originally a one-room house, the hallway and second room were added sometime later. The hall, built as a connecting room, is still a cold space as it would have been then, with storage possibilities for outerwear and foodstuffs. A washstand, mirror and homespun linen towels by the doorway continue to serve an overnight guest. In the second room an eighteenth-century trundle bed beckons those who might wish a softer, though less toasty, sleep. The rich-toned *ryijy* rug woven in this century, in an old pattern, and the icon that winks down from its candle-lit corner and white shroud stand diagonally across from the fireplace.

FROM
A HUMBLE
START

One of the sheds and the former main house were joined to create the living quarters. A Russian coin, dated 1803 and discovered in the foundation, shows the structures were renovated at least once before.

Porvoo is a picture-postcard town of Finland. Receiving its charter in 1346, the oldest part of town still keeps to the medieval plan, dominated by the massive limewashed fifteenth-century church and served by the river that was once its main boulevard. Bordering this frozen-in-time quarter of wooden houses, narrow streets and cobbled main square is a striking row of earth-red storehouses. One cluster of these *aittas*, or sheds, and the main house which had belonged to three generations of dyers was purchased some years ago by a local architect in the hopes of one day restoring them. Planning laws require that lots and original groupings of houses be kept

intact, challenging the renovator to conceptualize new living space from the series of small, joined structures that step up the river bank.

Hans Slangus made the most of the prized setting by giving attention to the central courtyard space which took its basic shape promptly with the addition of a new fence at streetside. He cut into the slope of the hill with short, broad flights of stairs and terraced planting areas that lead down to outdoor seating and small dock. Slabs of irregular flagstone embedded in the earth in a loose semicircle and mix-and-match iron and wood furniture painted traditional barn red and black, give a thoughtfully informal quality to

the yard. The whole reads like an open, breezy room and is used much that way in season.

A large glass door keeps the main room mindful of the historic placement and handsome usefulness of the eighteenth-century storehouses. The tone of its interior complements the surroundings without upstaging them. Here and throughout the rooms, a quiet combination of farmer's furniture and unpretentious new fittings done up in timeless ginghams and dulled paints is set off with bits of art, classic accessories and old ironwork, some of it found in the buildings. As outside, the success of the undecorated but well-groomed look is based on proportion, color and placement within the space, not precious materials or startling shapes. A large stuccco fireplace now takes the place of the open hearth in what was once the dyer's boiling room. Its solid volume acts as a positive, counterbalancing the negative open door space of similar dimensions.

Slangus handled the restoration

gently but firmly, introducing new flooring, walls and conveniences, but using simple materials which would feel at home here. Central stairs and unadorned door openings cut through and join the blocky structures, each one-room large, following along the natural grade of the hill. Wide pine floors and cocoa matting give boatlike tidiness to the riverfronted rooms. Built-in fittings are carefully detailed in a way that makes them disappear rather than stand out, reinforcing the owner-architect's view that the rehabilitation of buildings with such uncontrived design origins should speak softly of their new use, not shout for attention.

A boxy, white hearth dominates the living room. Bits of found ironwork decorate its surface above the fire box. Unmatched furniture is brought together with paint and plaid upholstery. In the study, central stairs are flanked by a desk on one side, bench and table on the other side. Woodwork in every room is brought into contrast by painting some elements and varnishing others to boat-like brilliance.

COUNTRY CHARM ON A MODEST SCALE

Delicate as the summer flowers blooming in the nearby gardens and fields are the furnishings in this wooden farmhouse that dates from the eighteenth century. The couple who live here—appreciators of fine music and antiques both by choice and by trade—have restored and brought gentle life to a place that has seen hardships and good times

in its two-hundred-year history. Built as a basic two-room home, the house is the last of the original farm buildings still standing. Of the others, only stone foundations can be found hidden in the grass around. A fire destroyed the last of the old structures as well as the pine forest that approached the lawn, but a grove of slender white birches later grew in the ashy soil. Now nature has fully reclaimed the prolific surroundings in this, an especially warm and sheltered part of the southern coast. Wild strawberries and bluebells make their bed beneath the birches; colorful mushrooms of all kinds pop up at summer's end, including the delectible trumpet-like chanterelles; elk graze quietly in open stands of trees.

The kitchen and side parlor belong to the oldest part of the house, with their log walls and ceilings intact. Wide-plank pine floors were just planed and scrubbed in the kitchen; exposed log walls were sealed and

This typical Finnish-red farmhouse has been expanded and renovated over the years. In the oldest part, built in the 18th century, log walls provide solid backdrop for a country pine hutch and Gustavian chairs that show Louis XVI influence.

reinsulated. Both here and in the other rooms which were added early in the nineteenth century, windowsills were built high to minimize drafts. The bulky kitchen oven is typical of its time and characteristic of southwest Finland. Most of the furnishings are antiques, fine-lined but sturdy and still fully usable: Gustavian furniture of Swedish/Finnish origin, a trio of early-nineteenth-century chandeliers, a set of rococo family chairs set round in different rooms and reupholstered accordingly. Pieces that had been dark were stripped to a light finish to complement a color scheme of pales that is cued to the old tile stoves in each room, as decorative as they are efficient. A trunkful of Russian crochet and lacework that was found in the attic adds frosting to the living rooms. Handwoven white runners on pine floors give a sense of fine but deliberate direction that organizes the space.

The side parlor and kitchen, far left, form the oldest wing. Furniture in both rooms was stripped to harmonize with the structure. Poles around the kitchen ceiling were used to hang baked breads. Painted 18th-century furniture from the Swedish/Finnish era decorates the living room and one bedroom. Rooms are balanced by symmetrical arrangements, linear linen runners. Brass and iron antiques fill pine tabletops and figure importantly in another bedroom, near left. Here a turn-of-the-century tile stove is one of four that still heat the house.

REGIONAL PRIDE AND LASTING CRAFT

This eighteenth-century log house escaped burnings by the German military in their retreat through northern Finland during the Second World War. The house that originally stood on this site did not. Piece by piece this 150-year-old structure was brought here and reassembled on what has always been, in Lapland, an ideal spot—by the banks of the Kemijoki River. When there were trails instead of roads, rivers served as the main routes of transportation, especially in the hinterlands. All those from one village even

traveled in a town-sized boat once a week to attend church and stowed the long vessel in a shed on the church grounds especially built for its storage.

The sturdy log house retains its original form and layout but was modernized to the extent that running water and electricity were installed. The kitchen has kept its place, just back of the entry hall which was typically a cold room, a sort of indoor vestibule. The main room is a large affair now used for working and dining, or sitting by the massive fireplace made in the

Houses that started with one square room were often expanded by adding others alongside. Here views through doorways show the effect; the owner's rag runners color the perspective. Lappish embroidered clothing hangs in the entry. Bags and shoes are made from reindeer fur or tanned hide; a lining of grass was used inside footwear as insulation. A root table and chair, 200 years old, show through the doorway.

regional style with built-in wood storage to one side and a pine seating surround framing the raised hearth. The house and its furnishings are as quietly true to their native soil and customs as are its owners, well-respected weaver and photographer, Elsa Montell-Saanio and Matti Saanio. They have carefully collected root furniture, simple tools and bits of natural decoration that would have well served the first owners of such a home. Colorful embroidered northern Lapp clothing spiritedly adorns the front hall and shelf. Dark winters and bright pride gave motivation for such decorative handwork; Eastern influences show in the heart and flower motifs and dense geometric borders.   Mrs. Montell-Saanio's own hand work softens log walls throughout, in much the same way as textiles historically have, as they were rotated around for different uses from table to wall to bed depending on the season or celebration at hand. All rag rugs, wall-hangings made by various techniques and curtains have been dyed and handwoven by her. Natural landscapes and religious symbolism dominate her figuratives; regional style and a preference for natural shades determine her colorings.

Local stone was used for the kitchen stove and the beehive fireplace. Whale bones and a chair carved from branches are unexpected living-room adornments. A bedroom has painted log walls, stenciled ceiling reproduced from original patterns and the owner's handwoven curtains. The long log house faces the river.

IN THE TRADITION OF THE TUPA

A satisfyingly square shape in schoolhouse red that stands in a meadow of Queen Anne's Lace is hardly what one envisions as shelter on the polar rim. Yet this child's-drawing-look-alike house sits snugly at the Arctic Circle offering the family that lives there all the charm of the naive and the convenience of the new. The house is an old flour mill

built near the banks of the largest lake of the region and was converted to its current use a few years ago under the guidance of architect, Yrjö Wiherheimo. His idea, to integrate strong shapes in contemporary furnishings with the heavy wooden exposed members of the existing mill, not only shows off the beauty of each in counterpoint but underlines the easy marriage of new and old forms in Finnish design. To save the appealing texture of the aged interior walls while protecting the weathered exterior, he chose to insulate the house on the outside using a layering of mineral wool and dead air space, finished off with vertical board and batten painted in traditional red with black trim. Modern multi-paned windows now hang in existing openings and repeat in small scale the square module of the house. Outbuildings on the property, once used for grains and other storage purposes, now serve as workspace and sheds, and absorb an overflow of gear belonging to sports-minded sons.

Inside, a clever organization of space stacks various activities and insulates first- and third-floor sleeping areas from each other by locating living rooms and kitchen between. In a plan that honors the integrity of the full-floor space of the main level, seating and dining areas adjoin each other

New furnishings, like the hanging chair designed in 1973 by Perttu Mentula, against old timbers set a best-of-both-worlds tone. Log outbuildings are now silvered with age.

Several of the furnishings are of Ritva Kellokumpu's design: the leather seating island and pillows in the living room, outline-quilted spreads and rag rug covers for their beds, a coffee table formed by standing drawer units back-to-back, and paper shades as closet doors/dividers in the master bedroom. Flush cabinets with no hardware and birch trim form a self-contained kitchen; exposed ductwork and log structure show above.

while the kitchen floats like a cube dropped into the room off to one side. Its neat navy-blue laminate walls trimmed in light birch enclose it like a wrapper but stop short of the ceiling, maintaining the continuity of the overhead wooden planks and beams. Wired-glass see-throughs pierce the navy walls for the passage of daylight and lightness of effect. As in old country houses the fireplace serves as pivotal point in the plan, but this is a modern one built of sheet metal to Wiherheimo's specifications by students from a local school. Heat-resistant glass sides and a raised hearth keep its glow in sight anywhere in the room.

"The house lives like a boat," says Jaakko Kellokumpu, its owner, obviously pleased. "We hear every gust of wind off the lake and all the systems that keep the place trim." Although the winds can blow cold and the snows here are deep, the systems of the house have been designed with the climate in mind. Exposed industrial ducting recycles hot air to warm the water that circulates through a clay tile floor downstairs. The heat that radiates from the floor and the sauna on that level rises back up through the house. Further, other details are shipshape, like the triple-glazed windows and solid-wood double doors.

AT HOME WITH HANDWORK

How a man works with materials gives him his identity and keeps him human. What makes a home personal is much the same: the things which fill its rooms give it its individuality and texture and ought to reflect those who live within. For Bertel Gardberg, one of Finland's foremost silversmiths and craftsmen, materials have always been important. His thoughts expressed, above, on what constitutes a home only seem surprising when one realizes that none of his own work has found a place in the cozy rooms he shares with his wife and children. Neither at first glance is there much sign of the clean modern forms for which he is known. Gardberg's house, like the man, proves his maxim: ask him about his designs and he'll show you mossy rocks in the forest that creeps in a friendly way up to his door. Inquire about his technique and he'll point out an old cow yoke or a rusted iron ship's ring. Like his conversation, his home speaks of his sources, not his current work, and of his humble admiration for beautiful objects shaped by other hands than his. He knows what many of his contemporaries seem to have forgotten: nature was the first shaper and designer for man. Long before a human being imagined what objects he could make, he simply selected from among the found forms in nature those which would serve his needs. "He chose with his hands, not his head," Gardberg reminds us, as he smoothes a rounded stone into which he has imbedded a bit of brass. Working with his hands is his way of staying in touch with that truth.

The Gardbergs' home is warm and inviting, filled with the uncomplicated things of different periods they both enjoy. Wooden furniture of honey-colored stain is predominant; some pieces were stripped down to their original finish, good painted pieces were touched up and left as is. Appreciation of what is has led them to an easy display of simple things: a rocker found in the house still takes its place by the fire, moss continues to fill seams in log joints of the walls. In a Finnish country armoire Irish sweet-shop jars sit by Russian earthenware and English porcelains. The small white coffeepot on its bottom shelf belonged to Mrs. Gardberg's ancestor, a

Traditional Finnish handwork decorates the living room: a painted chest with clock pediment, signed by a 19th-century cabinetmaker on the island of Björkö; a Renaissance table; Biedermeier chairs; rococo armoire; and rag rugs designed by Mrs. Gardberg. In his studio Bertel Gardberg works directly in stone, silver, metal or wood—sometimes in combination—without drawings. His tools and stools are as personal as his crafts work.

The armoire, made in 1770, was found with its original transparent blue stain inside, rosy tones outside. In the living room corner, pine chests mix with ship's art, family portraits, Finnish glass and textiles. The bedroom combines painted Petersburg rococo chairs, unusual Finnish pine cabriole-leg table, old wooden food boxes and Venetian glass chandelier.

country priest who first translated the Bible into Sami (the language of the Lapps) and in her words whose "schnapps glass was nearly as big as his coffeepot." Ship paintings, tools and sailor's art reflect Gardberg's love of the sea, nurtured since his boyhood on the coast, and his respect for the workings and design of nautical fittings.

Surrounding himself with things of the past frees Gardberg to seek ideas for his new work. And for him, these things give pleasure and fulfill the roles they always have. He believes in his surroundings as in his craft: "The proof of good design is that it can last forever."

ROMANTIC INTERLUDE

Shadows at midnight, candles at noon…Finland is a place where life alters in accordance with the dramatic change in light. Such images—one expressive of pale summer nights, one of short winter days—explain something of the juxtaposition of extremes by which every Finn lives. It is in this context that a deep love of nature in all her robes, from stark winter whites and grays to flowery summer greens, has always blossomed and flourishes today, and serves as a model for the romantic side of Finnish lifestyle.

Natural forms have always inspired the Finnish arts and crafts, architecture and design. Throughout their history, Finns have felt free to be guided by nature's flow and asymmetry, to bring her texture to life, to borrow from her symbolically in decorative pattern and relief work. The romance of the primitive, the lure of the wilderness, have traditionally held their place in the intellect and esthetic sense. Sometimes they are expressed obviously, as in the bears fashioned from granite that gaze down from a turn-of-the-century building facade; sometimes more subtly, as in the turf roof of a modern sauna which blooms in season with grass and clover. The ceremony of sauna and all-night celebration of Midsummer are examples of romantic Finland brought to life today. People are comfortable with such reference to their past, with bringing natural history forward in both symbol and ritual.

Other romantic reference points originated outside the country. The cross-currents of influence from the East and West have for centuries left their traces. Yet in their wake a characteristic Finnish way of life has always held its own, a style that has assimilated and simplified some of its borrowings from other cultures. A rich palette of deep colors, big rugged log houses with carved wood railings and trim, geometrically patterned textiles with primitive motifs, heavily ornamented pieces of ceramic and glass including some that sparkle with golden filigrane threads or meshwork…such are the decorative legacies from Byzantine Russia and the eastern Baltic. Indeed, Karelia (the Finnish province nearest to the Russian border) has been an important source of romantic design inspiration into this century. Many Karelians are of the Orthodox faith, like their Russian neighbors, and the mystique of its customs has long played a role in their decorative arts and dress. It was not unusual to see wooden icons with golden backgrounds twinkling from the dark loggy corners of Karelian homes.

Royal styles from Sweden and Imperial Russia filtered across borders bringing something of the glamour of court stylishness to their country neighbors, in the periods when each in turn claimed Finland as a duchy. At times architecture was commissioned by royal decree that changed the complexion of the Finnish townscapes in ways that are still in evidence today. In fact, Helsinki became the capital only when Czar Alexander I chose it for its proximity to St. Petersburg and gave it its fanciful pale-toned, neo-classical stamp by importing one of the best northern European architects of the day to draw plans for its state buildings. Antiques collected in contemporary homes largely owe their line to the tastes of Gustavus III, King of Sweden, whose European travels convinced him to order his own reinterpretations of French and English court styles for the royal premises and started a vogue for such furnishings in both Sweden and Finland. Today's pale schemes, white-painted furniture, side chairs and benches with Louis XVI-type detailing and delicately faceted chandeliers are romantic reminders of his courtly preferences.

But it was at the start of this century that the expression of the romantic reached its peak in the arts and design. Feelings of national pride were stirred by a growing administrative self-sufficiency; the Finns had developed higher economic and literacy levels at this time than their ruling neighbors, the Russians, and responded rebelliously to new political restraints. An interest had been kindled in ethnic roots when the national epic poem, the *Kalevala,* based on hundreds of folk tales from the Finnish pagan era, had been recorded by 1850 in its entirety by a traveling country doctor who tapped the memories and aural traditions of the peasants in the northeastern provinces. The richness of this extraordinary folk poem touched simple people and great artists alike in the spirit of the times and led to a national search for a style that was truly Finnish.

The resulting National Romantic style architecture is inviting and intriguing, massive in scale yet naively appealing in detail. Its development paralleled that of the Art Nouveau and Arts and Crafts movements on the Continent. In Finland, rusticated native gray granite and umber-stained log facades offer larger-than-life characterizations of forest wildlife, folkloric animal presences, backwoods vegetation and details from peasant architecture in three-dimensional splendor. The playful incorporation of these elements into city banks and state buildings as well as ordinary houses still stands today for the widespread welcome given a style that celebrated the unspoiled wilderness that much of Finland was and is. At the turn of the century the handicrafts flourished anew, unique craftswork was prized. The art of knotted woolen *ryijy* rug-making was revived for its decorative effect, beautiful pottery was fashioned, ceramic tilework became more ornamental, furniture showed influence of the British Arts and Crafts style.

An artful vision permeated life and set a creative romantic precedent still drawn on today. A method of setting up living space that incorporates the exotic, and a way of looking at life through nostalgic eyes are inheritances of this past. In the houses that follow, the selective revival of romantic looks and new ways of combining some of those elements are intriguing and inviting.

WELL-PRESERVED ELEGANCE IN A CHEKHOVIAN SETTING

The elegance of Czarist Russia, the grace of Royal Sweden—nowhere do the two meet with more polish than in manor houses of eastern Finland. Such homes are both meandering country properties and working farms, some first settled in grand style by Swedish families sent as reserve cavalry in the seventeenth century to reinforce the border against Russia, a traditional foe. Finland's history is, in part, a tale of this border.

Sun streams in through lacy curtains at Wehmais to fall both on Swedish Gustavian furniture gleaming white like the bleached linen runners that crisscross pine floors, and on warm-grained Russian Biedermeier furnishings silhouetted against hand-printed wallpapers brought over snow by sled from the nearest luxury town, then St. Petersburg. The mix is characteristic of the times and of a borderline landed gentry forced to take sides when Sweden lost the duchy to Russia. Those that remained, though of Swedish descent, were declaring themselves to be Finnish in loyalty. Such is the story of the family which has kept to their land here for three centuries. This, their present home, was built in the Finnish Empire style of the mid-1800s on the foundations of a previous family house. A veranda with the period look was added in this century.

Summertime here still finds the Russian samovar presiding on a sideboard of the shaded porch as it silently steeps tea to be served with home-baked pastries and meat pies. Life moves outdoors in the green months, as in the Chekhovian manner once common on both sides of the border, when the sweetness of the light nights and days is savored at the manor house. Yellow and white garden flowers perfume the air near stands of oaks, maples and fruit trees. Down by the lake smoke curls from the wood-fired sauna which has been lit to heat all afternoon so it is just right for the evening's

Islands of Swedish Gustavian furniture in the living room are separated by long linen runners laid to link the doorways. The runners were handloomed by the owner's mother who spun the linen from flax harvested on the farm, as was common at manor houses in the past.

In a sitting room (previous pages), hand-blocked wallpaper and Russian Biedermeier furniture were brought by sled from St. Petersburg. Original "Finland Album" scenes hang in series—one of the sets made of the new grand duchy by commission for Czar Alexander I in 1823. A guest room is furnished with Finnish Biedermeier, made by a local carpenter from Russian originals. The room was recently renovated.

bathing. Inside, the rooms are polished, the patina of their furnishings casting a comforting shadow of past over the well-restored present. In this generation the Russian wallpapers, a bit stiff with age, have been carefully reglued or stripped when irreparable. New rag runners were farm-loomed to complement wall and upholstery colors. The starched white linens with hand-crochet that give a finishing touch to nearly every room were redesigned in period style and made by villagers living nearby. In the kitchen, which has seen the most modernization over the years, the farm's old table and chairs are used for family breakfasts, and breads are still made in the great oven that used to be stoked only once for a full week's baking.

The Empire manor house has outbuildings in front; its veranda with awnings faces the garden out back. In a bedroom, black furniture is offset by white linens, embroidered pillows, a rich Russian carpet. The dining room, with its long china cabinets, adjoins the large farm kitchen. Groupings of furniture and family collections enliven corners of all the spacious rooms.

STARTING SMALL

The return to the home of one's childhood is a romantic journey. To come to own and renew such a place with both a respect for its simplicity and a feeling for its potential requires special understanding and a sensitive touch. Together, owner Kirsti Paakkanen and architect Ilkka Salo planned the conversion of the lakeside cottage where she grew up with her parents and sisters to a home in the country that is her retreat today. A warren of tiny rooms shared by many gave way to the luxury of open space filled with just

a few things of good quality. Most of the ceiling was removed revealing a peaked roof with pleasing proportions; rough planks above were finished off with new tongue-and-groove pine left natural in tone and sealed shiny with varnish. The four log walls which were structurally sound needed just some plugging and then were painted chalk white for relief against all the wood. A new floor was also laid in pine—a knotty red grade was chosen for use throughout as true to the house's simple country roots, and as

A straightforward facade belies the fanciful addition at the back, warmed up in winter with sheepskins for after skiing or skating. The cheerful outhouse is candlelit.

complement to its sleek new furnishings. The look today is polished and pristine, showing pride in its past and confidence in its future.

The conversion hinged on seeing new uses for familiar surroundings, on imagining new ways to provide for old needs without over-complicating the solution. A bedroom was created in a garret-like space above a new porch. Both have a splendid view of the treetops and the lake beyond. A modern kitchen was installed against one wall, ensuring convenience in minimal space. Electricity was brought into the house some years ago but water is

still pumped in from a nearby spring, and bathing takes place in a sauna down by the lake. Perhaps some things are best left unchanged (if a bit improved)—the wooden outhouse sits in a grove of trees and continues to offer one of the best undisturbed vistas in the place.

Opening up the interior gives a feeling of space and offers a glimpse of the intricate workmanship of the ceiling. Chandelier, sheepskins, the gleam of glass, the gloss of white leather add touches of unexpected luxury.

DESIGNER'S EYE, COLLECTORS' CHOICE

A love of travel and appreciation of fine craft have produced a worldly mix of collections in the home of Saara Hopea and Oppi Untracht. The extent of the melange is typified by the tablesetting laid for a summer-day's lunch: a modern table by Alvar Aalto pulls up to a nineteenth-century trundle bed/bench and a set of country shield-back chairs one hundred years older …an Art Nouveau style lamp hangs overhead…Japanese earthenware and German porcelain, Nepalese linens and Finnish stemware are set at each place…brass trays inlaid with silver from Damascus sparkle on the wall…all this while a chorus of Indian deities smile on from nearby. To name all the objects in sight would read like a map and miss the point of being transported into a space that manages to combine the lifestyle of the West and some mystery of the East. Untracht,

The glow of Asian metalwork and the sparkle of Russian icons remind us of their common roots in the East. Finnish Biedermeier desk and chairs blend handsomely. A brass samovar combines with exotic flora platter by Kaipiainen, Ms. Hopea's 1950s enamel spice jars, her silversmith-grandfather's hand-wrought mortar and pestle.

an international expert in jewelry and decorative metalwork, and Ms. Hopea, well-known for her glassware and jewelry designs, have travelled and lived around the globe. The educated ingenuity with which they combine their collections richly ornaments a modern two-bedroom apartment.

A sumptuous mix of objects in the open living/dining space is organized around Tibetan rugs in tones of deep blue and accents of orange that cover the floor in a patchwork layout. Shades of orange, ranging from tangerine to rust in nearly every room, balance the warm glow of metals, honey-toned woods, and sparkly icons. The delight is in the discovering and uncovering as one looks about. The ease with which objects from different cultures are combined and put to everyday use showcases them without distorting their design intent or value.

Ornamented Finnish pine—a trundle bench, above, and carved square chairs, at bottom—were suitors' wedding-gift handwork; country shield-back chairs show Hepplewhite influence. Ms. Hopea's own green glass design with cone-shape stem sits on the tabletop, below.

83

SPIRITED MANOR HOUSE COMBINES TASTE WITH SPUNK

Bökars is more than a manor house. It is the place where the spirit of Armi Ratia, founder and creative force behind Marimekko, still casts a magic spell over the old buildings that blink out at the Baltic through a scattering of birches. Here dinner is illuminated by the lustre of five chandeliers, one can bed down in a windmill or former granary, and

dancing on the lawn goes on 'til the seagulls fly in white clouds to land just before dawn. Bökars is a sleepy looking country house where textile designers, business acquaintances, friends, a professor in passing, the Ratia family of this generation...stay up late into the night chatting, strolling along

candlelit paths toward the sea, or sit in sauna and discuss politics or love.

If people make Bökars come alive, the stage has been set with great taste and good humor for an environment where one can enjoy the company of twenty-four guests on a weekend or draw away silently into a gazebo perched on rocks by the sea. Here, Armi created an

Bökars is a characteristic manor house with main building painted ochre, outbuildings earth-red or weathered-gray. The long cow barn is now a place for parties; the windmill and cottage have become quarters for overnight guests. Pine branches laid by the front door release their scent when feet are scraped. Inside, five chandeliers glitter in the dining room as one example of Armi's romantic daring. They were first hung from trees for outdoor parties.

atmosphere that presents possibilities but never dictates solutions. The main house is open and breezy, its generous tables accommodating many with ease. Furnishings are disparate pieces pulled together according to the eye of the house's late mistress; like the textiles for which she is known, the whole is clean and up-to-date but never dry. There are sturdy Finnish rockers all in a row, old painted cabinets from the west coast, grand piano, rocks piled on tables, cushions on the floor.

Every bedroom is a different color and has a different mood. As a guest one can choose the room that seems to fit. There is one that is delicate Gustavian, decorated with a four-poster bed, a crochet bedspread, a piece of Iris pottery from the once-famous works in nearby

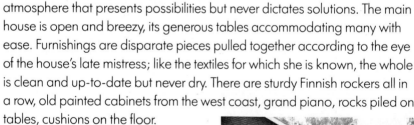

Porvoo. Another is all in wicker, with deep rose fabric walls and heavily draped tables. Great washes of color have been used to unite old furniture with new and give the rooms character.

The outbuildings all have different uses now, and most have beds tucked up in lofts overhead. The former dairy barn is a big dining room for parties of summer crayfish or Christmas cakes. Another barn has become a playhouse with great foam platforms and indoor swing that look out over

meadows. Everything changes with the season: summer tables set for pancakes and homemade strawberry jam move inside for winter when ice lanterns light the stairs and hot *glögg* is served before the fire. Colors and faces change, the feeling remains the same. As Armi used to say, "It is voices, lights, the aroma of baking bread, the smell of just-ironed linen that make the atmosphere of a home."

Unexpected combinations make the rooms special: crisp fabrics and antique furniture; painted walls and stripped ceilings, floors; big bouquets of garden flowers or fresh leaves in bold, clean-lined settings.

Each space changes character with its intended use and at the whim of its designer. One outbuilding was converted to a playhouse with foam platforms covered in bright Marimekko cotton. The guest bedroom is called "White Lady." In the hall, a new closet from antique doors is crowned with heather.

A ROMANTIC VIEW OF CONTEMPORARY LIFE

New Finnish upholstery and a table by Ben af Shultén meet old pine and international modern style chairs. Textural whites and naturals provide a clean canvas for 20th-century art and 18th-century metalwork.

A light space where people mix easily is set off with surfaces of well-worked wood, softly textured plaster and the dulled finish of antiques. "We wanted both a home for our sons and a setting for our art, and somehow a place where my husband could feel at sea," comments Irma Lillja about their Helsinki home. One does feel as if the water is lapping up around the deck off the living room. The sensation is achieved through a

two-level telescoping design with a large expanse of west-facing windows that offer clear views of the Baltic from almost every room. Such a setting is possible within the city limits.

Architect Ilkka Salo conceived of a contemporary scheme that borrows from the past in an interpretive and personal way. The would-be formality of rooms furnished with fine collections of old and new articles is pre-empted by an open plan that invites movement and daylight. At its hub is a plastered fireplace that freestands at the junction of three rooms, designed with soft curved edges to help the space flow. Cupola ceilings raise the roof over living and dining rooms, drawing the eye upward and breaking the formula of the white plaster and glass box. Their projecting form gives lightness to the rooms and makes pleasing interior allusion to the raised ceilings of Byzantine architecture. Clerestory windows at the cupola peaks throw soft light on stepped and mitred birch sides by day, warm white fluorescents bounce light up at the detailing giving a reversed effect at night.

A den in international style is warmed with a book collection housed in

shelves that wrap the room and break rhythm to encircle a soft leather sofa. As elsewhere, the sparkle of antique silver and brass, the gleam of polished marble and contemporary chrome bring shine to a background of white and natural materials. Light wood finishes give harmony to furniture of all styles. Loose all-white bouquets arranged by Mrs. Lillja freshen every space and add sentiment to even the sparer rooms. An open hearth reminiscent in form and texture of those found in homes since the 1600s has been reinterpreted in smaller scale and invites one to linger in the spacious kitchen.

Lighting plays a decisive role in casting a romantic glow over the blend of new and old furnishings. The lit cupola ceiling of the living room plays up its soft birch sides; lamps in the bedroom warm the wood ceiling and a collection of gilt frames in contrasting scales.

ARTIST'S PLAY ON MATERIALS

A scattering of Ms. Pullinen's sculpture can be seen here both inside and out. She works in marble, bronze, plastic and sometimes fiber. A stone grain storehouse on the property will become her studio.

Laila Pullinen's home is the unassuming farmer's house that belonged to a manor house destroyed by fire. All that remains from the grander building are its gold leaf valences and fineals which were treated to dramatic new draperies made of yards of unbleached muslin by Ms. Pullinen. Most of the furnishings owe their present appearance to her touch—they have been stripped, painted, sewn, woven or reconstructed by

her. Such doings might qualify as light work to the small blonde woman used to wielding her own blow torch and other heavy equipment for her sizeable bronzes and marble sculptures. Her husband, a doctor, arranges all the flowers for their home.

That they now live in the simplest of the houses from the estate suits Ms. Pullinen. A Karelian by birth, she learned to live lean through years of skirmishes in that province; she and her family left everything and evacuated like some 400,000 other Finns in the aftermath of World War II when most of Karelia was annexed to Russia. A marble sphere on the living room floor among other examples of her work is part of a series called *Freedom*. Its more obvious rolling stone imagery is superseded in the sculptor's mind by her thought that, "To be free you must be hard as stone—if someone wants

A generous use of fabric relaxes the strong lines of the interior. Lengths of muslin are draped under gold-leaf valences at upstairs windows, and the fabric headboard of the master bedroom recalls the artist's paper collages. For the dining room, early Aalto stacking chairs were a find, later treated to several coats of black enamel. In the corner, a 17th-century Italian cherub looks down on Ms. Pullinen's portrait of a Finnish male: a delicate mandolin sits inside a rugged, oversized cello case.

to kick you, he breaks his foot and you are unharmed."

The interior of the house is a chiaroscuro of rough and smooth. Pine boards laid bare and whitewashed after the wallboard was stripped away (this effect as a result of the sculptor's return to the demolition site one day to find that she liked the look), exposed brick pillars and jags of uneven plaster that do not quite meet the ceiling line form the background against which Finnish and Italian modern furnishings, smooth marble tables and velvet cushions are set. Other pieces are discards salvaged from here and there and refinished, like the now classic Aalto stacking chairs that are used for dining and a nineteenth-century studio table from the Ateneum, Helsinki's fine-arts school and museum. Ms. Pullinen likes to assemble unmatched parts to form a new whole. Their "canopy" bed is made from timbers wrapped in canvas and its headboard is a fabric version of her paper collage theme. When her husband suggested that a proper master bedroom should have a chandelier, she bought antique-shop crystal and braid and created one around the naked overhead lightbulb. But through her play on materials runs a thread of symbolism that also unifies her art: "The spirit is the message. My work is never abstract in pure form. My wish is that there will always be some poetry behind it."

IN THE SPIRIT OF AN OLD HUNTING LODGE

The building of a log house today is tempered by the risk that the results will be corny or clunky. This log house built on the southern coast is neither. Its dusky interior and heavy furnishings give it a spirited richness that harkens back to the feeling of an old Russian hunting lodge.

Log houses are as old as the earliest existing Finnish buildings. A specialized method of building with logs developed in Lapland, however, where the pines grow even more

On a wooded site with a rocky slope that leads to the sea sits this contemporary log and glass house. The dark new space easily accepts sturdy fittings from yesterday and today.

slowly than in the south of Finland because of the severe climate. These trees are characteristically harder than those of the south (which are in turn denser and harder than those of southern Europe and America) and some tend to spiral in the forest as they grow old. When these die, still standing, they drop their bark and needles and turn a lovely weathered gray. The technique of building with such wood was perfected by northern hunters and woodsmen who found they could build with these trees, hundreds of years old, immediately after cutting since they had died and dried upright. In planning such a house, one visualizes the results from the inside out; that is, because logs are naturally of varying widths and trees are broader at their bases than at the tops, the plans for the house must be followed as they specify the inside measurements. The outside dimensions can vary many centimeters with the sizes of the trees used.

The construction of this house departs from tradition in that it makes use of modern technology: the structure is steel-supported and clothed in logs to permit design possibilities including window openings that visually break the mass and bring the surrounding forest in. Open beams and peaked roofline help give an airiness to the inside space and finish in deep overhangs outside that shelter porches and entry. Inside, log ends are left exposed where walls meet, calling attention to the primitive construction and continuity of this single-log-deep building method where one material does the job of both supporting and insulating the house. A gray Norwegian stone was chosen for the fireplace as its color and bulk harmonize with the logs.

Heavy furniture feels right in such a setting, its strong forms a match for the weighty walls. Some furnishings date back to the late 1600s; the Finnish Renaissance dining chairs and table are the oldest. A large farmhouse armoire, whose light wood contrasts handsomely in the living room, comes from Ostrobothnia on the west coast where carpentry has always been of high repute. Rocking chairs, stripped of dark paint, balance the armoire across the room; their style was influenced by the Boston rocker that created a stir in Finland during the late eighteenth century. Boston-type rockers were made on the Bothnian coast and even became the rage amongst worldly Russians who imported them from the grand duchy to St. Petersburg. Other treasures that decorate the rooms include a leather desk chair from Mannerheim's house (Finland's highly respected field marshal and army commander), family heirlooms from homes in Viipuri, and a bearskin rug left by a grandfather. Warm candlelight is everywhere in coach lamps and candelabra, and mysteriously magnified behind water jugs.

Living-room surfaces range from stone to stripped pine, styles from early-19th-century rococo candlesticks to modern geometric cottons. A balcony faces out to sea; it serves as a seating area for after sauna.

The dining room's painted cabinet dates from the early 1800s. Tables and chairs are Finnish Renaissance; copper and brass are from Finland and Russia. In a bedroom, below, is a not-so-serious mix of 18th-century furnishings.

Candleglow is magnified behind globes of water. An Art Nouveau lamp and Field Marshal Mannerheim's desk chair enhance a quiet study.

LIVING IN A
WORLD OF WHIMSY

Imagine a forest of pansies or pomegranates or seed pods as big as pines, and clocks that bloom and drifting keyholes that beckon. Such is the fantasy in ceramic that is the world of Birger Kaipiainen. In his apartment, as in the painted porcelain platters of this design, mysterious landscapes emerge

where intense color teases against patches of white and black, unexpected scale creates new relationships and forms mix easily from any place and time. "Everything is possible," Kaipiainen offers.

The rooms where he lives are filled with veranda lamps, mirrors in golden icon frames now reflecting back the gazer's face, a royal bedstead, collected bits of crystal from an Orthodox island cloister in what used to be Finnish Karelia. Personal mementos and found objects, gifts from artist friends—all find a place in a small home that reads much like the collections

Kaipiainen's playful assemblages personalize the space: on a table, Napoleon III ornamental metallic fruit and miniature furniture including his so-dubbed "smallest chair in the world" in silver from Georg Jensen; Polish royal bedstead hung with Marimekko cotton; lithograph in embossed paper frame of the Czar's summer palace, with mirror writing at top; silver crochet table runner; period, provincial and fantasy-painted furniture.

of dolls' furniture arranged on some of the tabletops. Good examples of Gustavian salon furniture and griffen-adorned Empire benches stand near an old peasant hutch and pieces of hand-me-down furniture painted some years ago by Kaipiainen with tassels and swags, ladies' faces and *faux* forms from fancier period

pieces. Kaipiainen is at once a fragile creature who loves ballet (he has been to more than two hundred performances of Swan Lake) and borrows from its imagery occasionally for his work, and a devilish spirit who answers questions with a cheshire-cat-like grin and a nod, and who might mysteriously disappear from a country weekend in the middle of the night. His bedroom is night sky blue, his living room sunny yellow—the arrangements within them quite without pretension. The hutch, intended as a corner piece, turns one of its sides against a wall (there was no corner that would do) exposing the other side for trinkets and dried bouquets, photographs of an admired Russian ballerina and an Orthodox saint. The artist lives very much as he likes, affected by people and experiences that please him. He acknowledges Finland's cultural good fortune to feel influences from both the East and the West, savoring this happy circumstance with an exceptional Finnish mix of logic and whimsy.

MODERN MANNER

The surprise of Finnish modern design is that the best of it shows few of the characteristics for which modernism is nowadays fashionably derided—traits like coldness, austerity and rigidity. Its warmth makes it approachable; its balance and restraint make it elegant. For in the Finnish manner, modern manages to be up-to-date without forgetting its country and romantic legacies. In effect, an attraction of opposites gives the style its long-lasting appeal both within Finland and outside. The result is a look that is at the same time primitive and sophisticated, earthy and fine, popular and artful, new and lasting.

The seeds of modern were planted early in Finland—and at a crucial time. During the liberating first years of this century, when the emergence of an individualized national style heralded Finland's growing independence, a precedent was set for high design standards and for great respect due the architect and designer/craftsman of the day as shapers of national destiny. Growing industrialization placed a burden on the agrarian culture to respond to new needs for housing in developing urban centers. Architects and designers were called upon by citizens' groups, by various design organizations formed in the late nineteenth century and, finally, by the new republic to draw up solutions. The concept of town planning was taken up. Every person was deemed to have a right to decent living space, sanitary conditions, climate-proof construction, daylight and greenery. Finland had no class-bound history to restrict her development of these modern notions, never a feudal system, nor royalty within her borders. The country took rather naturally to easing her growing pains in free-thinking ways and challenged designers to think of the community at large almost from the start.

Even as the more decorative National Romantic and Art Nouveau styles were flourishing, another school of thought was calling for innovation and simplification—in line with the most contemporary international thinking. So clear was the message that it proved instrumental in causing Eliel Saarinen to streamline his work, smoothing its transition from romantic to modern. Architect Gustav Strengell was vocal and his ideas foreshadowed the functionalist principles which were to become dominant by the 1930s. In 1901 he wrote, "Beauty…in no wise [way] consists of haphazard external ornamentation….A chair is beautiful when it fulfills its function to the highest degree. It can lack all ornamentation so long as it is comfortable and constructed so that the function of each part is clearly apparent."

By 1929 a young Alvar Aalto had designed his landmark chair for the Paimio Sanitorium. To make it, he had perfected a system of bending plywood, using the wood's own moisture, yielding a shape that was beautifully organic yet reproducible in quantity. The Paimio chair most recognizably symbolizes the early realization of the functionalist ideal in Finland's mass furniture production. Interestingly, the earliest peasant chairs carved from stumps or tree roots, made for one-room log houses and still very much in use in the countryside at this time, also then qualified as beautiful by Strengell's definition. In Finland, the esthetic link between primitive and modern was direct. Like the peasants (and unlike southern European architects fascinated by tubular steel and glass) Aalto worked mainly in wood, in appreciation of its warmth to the eye and to the touch.

The preference for natural materials was maintained through the 1950s—peak years for the modern style, when Finnish designers won more than their expected share of awards at the Milan international design fairs, and names like Tapio Wirkkala and Timo Sarpaneva became known worldwide. The 1930s and 1940s had been fertile decades for the ripening of ideas. A vision grew as the crafts/folk ethic found new application in the functionalist philosophy, and technology made ready to interpret the blend. In spite of the destruction and scarcity imposed by the war years (or in response to them) Finland found herself able to both build her image and rebuild the country, causes which worked off each other during the following decades.

The Finnish challenge is to look forward while thinking back, to work with time-tested materials in ever new ways. Today, while houses are roomier with fine, open plans, they are still mostly wood-constructed and not wasteful of space. The look is a clean, fresh mix of pure shapes and simple materials that are made well—to last. Up-to-the-minute conveniences sometimes sit comfortably side by side with what some of us consider old-world luxuries: heated tile floors and towel bars share space with streamlined bathroom fittings; sleek black-glass cooktops may keep kitchen company with wood-fired iron ovens. There is an admirable understatement about the look and little fear of the unembellished surface, the unfilled space. Spareness comes intuitively to these northern people, yet so does warmth in spirit and design. White walls and wood tones make up the simple interior landscape against which people and objects create splashes of color—much the same as in the Nordic outdoors.

Nearly a century of modern attitude, enriched by concern for the common good and respect for artistic tradition, has created a high standard of expectation in living design among Finns today. Woodworking is executed with the care of fine cabinetry for saunas and window frames, as for furniture and accessories. A glass vase is shaped so that it will be beautiful as a container for summer flowers, but also as an object that can stand empty in winter, like sculpture. In modern terms, characteristic Finnish simplicity and respect for use become virtues. When design stands on its own without heavy decoration, its form is laid bare. Its quality depends on infallible proportion, excellent materials and skillful production. In meeting this challenge Finnish modern has become classic.

ROMANTIC REASONING, FUNCTIONAL EXPRESSION

Often one does the right thing spontaneously," suggests Kaija Siren in evaluating how she and her husband Heikki, both architects, developed plans for their own house. "We were always doing our own work in such a hurry that we just found the house this way after awhile." The house, although thought out, was not exactly planned as a whole. It grew. What started as a design that would provide living space for them and an office for their then small firm, enlarged itself in two later stages as both their family and business needs warranted. At first, practical needs were met by a postwar solution: in 1951 the decision to have one structure serve two roles was partly an economic one. So was the choice to use simple available materials like native wood and brick. The Sirens decided on a design where living and work were co-joined but housed in their own wings: the peaked main portion provided for all family needs, a flat-roofed section stepped down the sloped site and was used as office space. Facing the street side is the high-pitched black

The structures were planned to relate to the site and existing vegetation. A high-peaked roof disappears amid tall trees. A lower addition is balanced by a strong horizontal wall at the street side.

Different rooms create different moods, with styles reflecting various phases of the house's expansion. The original entry hall is spare with an appealing balance of elements in natural materials. The living-room ceiling line is called out with wood; it turns down at the window wall to form a fascia. Other rooms were converted from office to second living room, from dining to conference room. Sailing memorabilia hangs in Heikki Siren's study.

slate roof that reaches low, a dark surface that was intended to make the building look smaller and disappear into nature. "Perhaps our idea was romantic, but the solution was functional," adds Heikki Siren.

Additions were made in 1956 and 1966, and then ironically when the space was its largest the four children were grown and moved out and so did the office, to its own building next door. Now, as their home, it works well for conferences or a houseful.of grandchildren. The Sirens found that the house felt quite comfortable, and that they preferred the ordinary materials

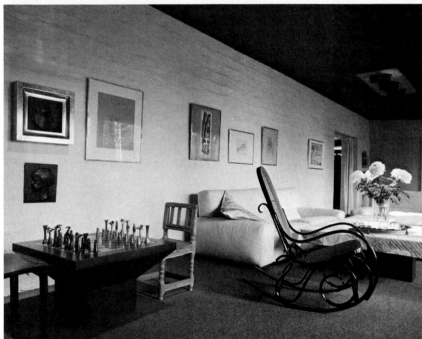

and the warmth those naturals brought to their functional solution.

As the house expanded the architects continued to specify brick walls lightly washed over with plaster, Finnish pine ceilings, clay floors and furniture covered in cotton. To these they have added personal belongings that speak of their love of sailing, family and a life of shared work. The older parts of the house can be indentified by the fine-lined early modern character of their design work and furnishings. Other rooms have become a collage of things brought back from travels in the Middle East, the sculpture of their son-in-law Zoltan Popovits, and their art collection. Mementos of J. S. Siren—Heikki's architect-father and teacher to both of them, whose best-known work is the parliament building in Helsinki—find a place here too. Throughout, it is a house with strong perspective and soft light. On the newer side, an expanse of glass shows the Sirens' characteristic use of bronzed steel-frame windows that impose a pleasing grid on the wall and grounds it faces.

THROWING NATURE A CURVE

Some house layouts state rather clearly how their rooms are to be used, by whom and during which parts of the day. This house makes no such demands but does ask of the people who live here or are invited that they be part of a group and conscious of everyone's need to find a place within a common space. So when children are present the adults must accommodate their play, when a meeting is held others must respect it. It is a house that encourages the integration of family and a sharing of activities. Interior

The Kukkapuro house sits in a forested community fifteen minutes outside Helsinki. The fine-lined window grid and bright exterior panels contrast crisply with blanketing snow and call to mind the color composition of a Mondrian painting.

architect Yrjö Kukkapuro has always worked at home, a lifestyle he continues to maintain with his artist-wife Irmeli: "We do not feel we are working at home, but rather that we are sleeping in our studio—and that is a feeling we enjoy because we like our work," says Kukkapuro. He cites a childhood of living in a three-room apartment with his parents, four brothers and sisters and his grandmother as one of the reasons he is not fond of closed doors.

Such a swooping shape looks a bit like an unidentified object that just landed in a clearing in the forest, its bright colors broadcasting the news through snowy surroundings. It is a house of the sixties, reminiscent of a time when its owners, as artists, were interested in new forms, machines that held promise and man-made materials. Together with engineer and architect, Eero Paloheimo, they planned this graceful house whose dimensionality is dependent on the tension of a triangular mass of steel-framed concrete fixed at three points. The interior of the concrete shell is sprayed with polyurethane

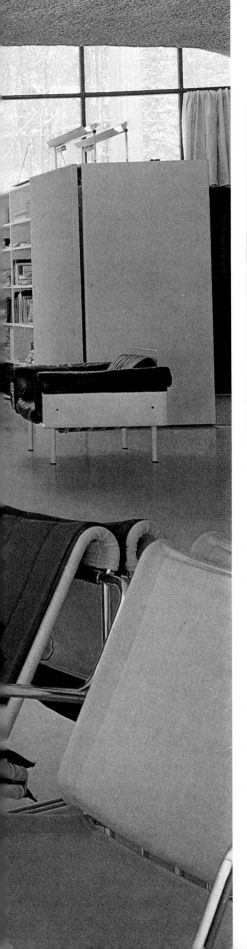

foam; its exterior is covered by a flexible roofing of bituminous rubber. The materials breathe, so the house may expand or contract with the climate.

"It was a time we were fascinated by the capsule shape," recalls Kukkapuro. "At first that was the only form we used to break the openness of the interior space." He had two plastic capsules made to delineate the bathing area and enclose its functions. Color was keyed to changes in use and manipulated to create different perceptions of depth as in a modern painting. Later, practicality dictated the building of walls to close off the two sleeping areas (although an all-round transom window arrangement keeps them light) and movable dividers were brought in to fashion pie-shaped studio spaces that stand open to the central living space.

A tidy work island is the only clue to the kitchen, whose very complete rear storage wall and built-in systems allow it to float in much the same way as the gallery-like grouping of furniture, all of his design. Such an open landscape allows complete freedom of rearrangement for a meeting or a dinner, or the change of seasons. In winter, activities are more centrally oriented as the snowy-white environment lightens and brightens the house through walls of windows. In summer, the interior is shady, reflecting the green of a mature deciduous forest. At that time the dining table (that splits into modular halves) might be moved to catch the breeze at the open doorway. That such a pristine environment can also feel very human is a tribute to the excellence in scale and comfort offered by both the house and Kukkapuro's award-winning furniture designs. But more than that, it has to do with two artists' clarity of vision and warm, personal lifestyle.

The open multi-use space is the core of a house where only the kitchen is fixed; all other furniture moves according to use and taste. Divider walls demark both of the Kukkapuros' studios, entry and bathing area.

Blacks and whites reinforce the geometry of dining and cooking areas. Furniture and lighting are of Kukkapuro's design. A storage wall plus work-island make a kitchen.

The pure shape of the late Kyllikki Salmenhaara's ceramic cups with sandwich boards feel at home in the clean lines and handsome proportions of the space. Below, is the architect's studio with the cardboard drawer and file system of his design.

Side-by-side capsules are for shower and toilet; they block the steel sink from view.

PRECISE STATEMENT
WITH A SLEEK FINISH

If a design book on Finland were to be subtitled "1001 Ways to Work in Wood," this house might head the chapter on new care in detailing. Built in central Finland in a well-preserved neighborhood of simple painted neo-classical houses that date from the early 1900s, it had to abide by that exterior style. Its owners added to the town requirements their personal preference for three small bedrooms, sauna, fireplace and a plan that would maximize the lake view, in their discussions with architect Ilkka Salo. The completed house is an exercise in precision of woodwork and sleekness of form with a facade that steps in and out sensitively to incorporate all functions under an unbroken roofline. To accomplish this task and to make the most of lake frontage, the slim house runs the full width of its lot and sits close to the relatively quiet street. At street side its cream and white panelling give it a reserve befitting the surroundings. Only the breezeway that pierces its calm facade alludes, when its gates stand open, to the painterly landscape within. The passageway technique of connecting the public and private spaces was inspired by the style of houses in Naantali, an old west-coast fishing village.

The morning-sun-washed exterior of the house is counterbalanced by a cool no-color scheme inside. Here, pine floors and ceilings become sophisticated and slick, stained deep gray-brown. The shade selected for the smooth high-gloss floor was diluted down a stop and used in matte finish for the tongue-and-groove ceiling that runs along the opposite grain. A coil system installed behind ceiling boards radiates heat down evenly, giving a sensation of warmness from overhead sun. Absorbing its warmth, the dark floor is always comfortable underfoot and helps in the equitable distribution of heat. International style furnishings in tones of charcoal to black appear like shapes that grow up from the dark base and read in silhouette against chalk-white walls and windows which orient the main room toward the lake. A perfectly planned pullman kitchen, bedrooms whose efficient built-in storage cuts down on room size and scaled-down den with requisite open hearth, allow the living/dining room the luxury of open floor space and a ceiling that measures six meters at its spine.

The living room, with its low profiles and high ceiling, is furnished with predominantly Italian modern furniture and lighting, a Ritva Tulonen sculpture hanging from above, and a Riihikoski painting on the sofa wall.

Interior and exterior vistas are given by a precision plan: Pullman kitchen, tunnel-passageway that leads from street to lawn and lake, doorway from the den to an expansive deck.

FINE LINES AND BOLD STROKES

One in a group of five connected terrace houses, this was designed in 1959 by Kaija and Heikki Siren as part of the garden-city Tapiola, twenty minutes from downtown Helsinki. After World War II, the Finns responded to an increased need for housing as they had in the past, with town planning. This time the concept was taken farther—in terms of allotted area (575 acres) and expected population (15,000), dedication to a full mix of cultural offerings and services and general excellence in architecture—resulting in

Dark-framed, single-pane windows make nature paintings of the surroundings. Blacks and whites integrate chairs and sailors' chests from the 1600s with modern Finnish and Italian furniture.

an exemplary blend of functionalism and sensitivity to nature. The plan has proven itself to be not only community responsive in terms of schools, churches, shops, offices and varied housing but has maintained the natural environment so that its lake offers sailing, its sloped terrain cross-country skiing, and its tall trees and winding paths general enjoyment of the outdoors for everyone who lives there.

The interior of this house seems to have taken its cue from the white brick and dark charcoal facades of the elegant joined-home plan. The architects' solution, to offset the houses in two groupings and step them down a slope, draws nature in to an even greater extent, forming roof gardens and interior courtyards for each. The black and white exterior was settled on for its integration amongst white birch and fir trees, and stark snowy landscapes in winter. When the current owners moved here three years ago they felt themselves fully receptive to the clean-lined, well-lit setting and traded in their heavy Art Nouveau style antiques for modern furnishings.

This is a house that lives bigger than it looks, making its interior surprising in all that it offers: sauna, four bedrooms, three seating areas, two outdoor living spaces and expanses of windows and doors that link nearly all these rooms to a courtyard or roof deck. Custom cabinetry original to the house eliminates the need for extra furniture and saves floor space. A bold black-strokes-on-white decorating scheme stands up to the striking graphic lines set by bronzed-frame windows, cast-iron circular staircase and white ceramic-tile floors. Strong furnishings of all styles—from Finnish Renaissance to Italian modern—combine with no loss of character. The owners enjoy all the possibilities offered by the well-thought-out plan: an evening with friends will see cocktails served on the white banquettes, a simple meal transported to the upstairs dining area (with its own small grill and open deck and nearby sauna), and coffee taken in the comfortable main living room in front of the fire.

The ground-level front door opens to a graphic view of tiled stairs and a cast-iron spiral staircase, cut by a strategically placed marble bust. Window walls to exterior and to interior corridors allow for light-filled rooms with outside views. At top is a sculpture by Marru Wirkkala.

SITTING LOW ON A BROAD HORIZON

A high-tech interpretation of the Finnish box-shaped house is the home and studio of architect Antti Nurmesniemi and his wife Vuokko, a textile designer. Their desire, as traditional as it is modern, was to combine work and living under one roof in a plan that gives visual communication between the spaces. An open-plan house, where changes in level or surface materials offer the only separations between areas (except for sleeping or bathing) and clear glass partitions unite living room with office space, refuses compartmentalization just like their lifestyle.

The steel-framed glass and wood box sits on a foundation partly dug out of the ground, allowing it to rest as close as possible to the horizon line. The idea was that the house should not be intrusive on the skyline (although codes would have allowed a higher structure in that place), but that it should be pleasing from the outside as well as from the inside. So while the house is

This box-shaped house, interpreted in glass and steel, sits low on the horizon and makes for open, light-filled space inside. The Nurmesniemis' own furniture and fabric designs furnish the rooms.

125

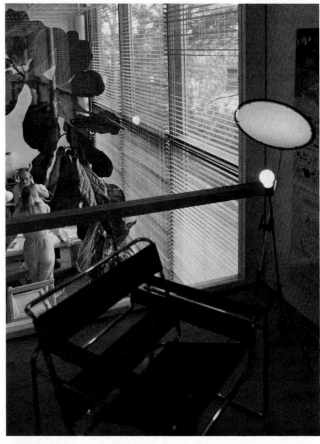

neutral or reflective from the exterior, its interior space is very much enriched by the nature that surrounds it. Older trees on the site, which were conserved during construction, are brought into view from every level giving it a rare advantage over most city houses. Further, just as the water is responsive to those things around it, this house is sensitive to the sea's changes and reflections. By virtue of its siting and materials, the structure lives with a rhythm of its own. The bedroom is situated so it gets morning light; as the sun arcs around, it gives the living levels a glow, softly striping the rooms through blinds made of pine.

Nurmesniemi's furniture designs maximize the striped effect of Vuokko's bold textiles and both reinforce the strong horizontality of the house. The patterning of the overhead strutwork, library shelves, ceramic-tile surfaces and wood-framed windows conforms to the cubic design. An extensive use of natural materials and especially of pine deepened in tone by the sun, gives a living breathing quality to a generously scaled interior furnished with strong forms. A pine ceiling is brought lower on the bottom level to give intimacy to a seating area that adjoins an indoor pool.

Life in a glass box is warmed with wood and artful arrangements of cut green leaves and plants. Open levels are complemented by an enclosed sauna and pool area, and an intimate space with its long stretch of sofa and collection of shoes for relaxing after bathing. Antti Nurmesniemi designed, among other pieces, the sauna stools and the tripod lamp near an interior window that overlooks the adjoining architecture studio.

EASY ASSEMBLY OF CURRENT FAVORITES

The easy-going apartment of Timo Vesara shows his interest in objects, especially those of his colleagues' design. Combined with a sense of humor and a sense of self, the pieces are international with an underlayment of Finnish style. Vesara, a consultant in the design community, has received some pieces as gifts, others as cast-off prototypes—special to him in that they often do not conform to the lines of the final products. Some things he has collected as work he admires, some are expectedly the design of clients. Some are found objects. The quirky character of this National Romantic style apartment building seemed to him to call for such a treatment, rather than a built-in or straight one-note modern scheme.

The handsome glazed tile stove, pine floors and white plaster walls are all in fine shape and original to the building. Vesara planned the apartment with the stove in mind, but notes that its real beauty is that it does not dictate any interior scheme. The stove is handmade showing early-twentieth-century detailing and rich hand-coloring, but the green solid tones and self-contained form allow an admixture of almost any style from this century.

Black and white with small splashes of color make for a look in the apartment that is precise but inviting with its assortment of shapes. Warm sun bathes the rooms at different times of day bleaching out some surfaces so they blend with the walls, drawing others into shadow and reinforcing their cool. Vesara has carved his office area out of a bit of the bricked-in basement that he rents downstairs. There he has whitewashed its uneven walls to bring out the texture; more light and shadow is thrown by means of square windows set in the deep relief of the heavy walls.

The living room juxtaposes a Bellini sofa, Cimano table, Maurer lamps, Kukkapuro chair and Ratia cube system. Vesara's own watercolor of the National Romantic apartment building hangs nearby.

A bits-and-pieces approach to decorating combines a new office chair by Heikkilä and Wiherheimo with a sawhorse-desk and cube surround; fishing lures are suspended near a fan on a tripod; a wooden skid becomes a radiator cover.

A LANGUAGE OF FORMS

My view of art is narrow, very strict. That way when someone calls me, they call because they want what I do and they know what they will get —something white!" Simo Heikkilä's work is not completely without color (or humor), but he prefers measured doses. His interest, as an interior architect, lies in forms—in a simplified language of form reduced to its basic elements. He explains, "Even a wire can be used decoratively. When it hangs free it forms a natural line. If you like, you can really enjoy such simple language." Wiry is how the chair designed by Heikkilä and Yrjö Wiherheimo might be described, an example of which stands in the owner's living room as well as in the design collection at the Victoria and Albert Museum in London.

Heikkilä likes to give identity to each object with which he works. Each element in his apartment shows completion and is given space so it can be seen on its own as well as part of the interior. Even a window blind is installed projecting out from the wall so its dimensionality is forced. Not only can it be manipulated to give more or less depth to the slats but it also admits daylight from all sides, and casts its own shadow against the wall when inside lamps are lit. He has placed it in its own plane like other things in the rooms. Heikkilä also uses contrast to give identity. He avoids using two light woods in one room.

Open spaces furnished with only a few things call attention to Heikkilä's personal choice of objects. A line-up of black leather and chrome chairs in the living room is a design of his teacher Yrjö Kukkapuro, and no doubt serve as inspiration in his own work. An appreciation for the simplicity of Oriental solutions is seen in the small Chinese folding chair on one side of the room and in a stack of grass cushions used often as seating. His bathroom design shows the same minimal style harmony as in the Japanese esthetic.

Honest chair shapes, three by Yrjö Kukkapuro, above, an old cottage-industry-made design by Muurame, below, are highlighted by spare room treatment, with Heikkilä's stereo

speaker, desk and table designs . An all-in-one bath plan with a center drain allows for no separation between the shower and the rest of the floor.

CONTEMPORARY COUNTRY

Although the concept of town planning had been accepted in Finland by the late nineteenth century as a way to accommodate the shift of the working population to the industrial cities, it was in the early years of this century that the idea bore fruit in the more beautiful garden town plans. In 1920, just three years after independence was won, construction in the Käpylä area of Helsinki was begun in the neo-classical style popular at the time. Not only was Käpylä innovative in building goals and techniques —165 residential one- and two-story structures comprised the grouping of simple apartments and detached houses, each with its own vegetable garden—but it managed to borrow from English and Italian town concepts and restate their principles in the language of the Finnish vernacular in form and color. More than that, it became the first, and still is one of the most charming, examples of a full-service community that shares utilities and sauna, shops and school.

A minimal approach to the living-room layout uses graphic arts and lean furniture forms in deliberately strict fashion. The foreground chair is Heikkilä's design with Yrjö Wiherheimo.

The all-white stairwell turns treads at a midway landing where small sailboats help to define the no-contrast space. An old country bench joins a modern table, chairs and textiles to form an eating area. Bouquets of field flowers are arranged freestyle and dry in great bunches overhead.

The shady lanes and green yards of Käpylä clearly instill a feeling of country in contemporary Helsinki life. By a special arrangement, houses and apartments here are privately owned, but the land is leased, so the city sees to the continuity of its services and outward appearance. Nevertheless, one is at liberty to make of his adjacent grounds what he likes, giving each house an individual stamp. The yard of the Salovaara house is a delightful combination of tended and free. Amidst dirt paths and grass, white-petaled apple blossoms and purple lilacs are followed by garden flowers and herbs as summer ripens. Inside, the same informal attitude persists. Good planning is there: built-in banquettes and bookcases, functional Aalto furniture and modular cabinets make a bedroom suitable for both sleeping and work; but the mood is warm and easy and friends are as likely to sit around the kitchen table talking as wander into the living room onto which it opens.

Its owners removed three small doorways to make the spaces connect. Theirs is a postwar generation's attitude to keep windows and doors open throughout the house, making all environments accessible and visually attuned. Cotton fabrics designed by Vuokko—one of Finland's outstanding modern textile artists—are used to give unity to the rooms. Päivikki Salovaara, press attaché for Vuokko, designed her own furniture and fabric treatments. For a change of tone she rotates textiles, and accents become red against the whites and pale naturals. Painted planked ceilings, original floors and corner stoves take the edge off streamlined modern furniture and contribute to an atmosphere that seems effortless and comfortable, as the now highly desirable "workers' housing" was meant to be.

Outdoor advantages to life in the city for Käpylä residents include garden plots and yards, plus now-mature trees. Indoors, unassuming custom pieces and modern classics make a sitting room out of the bedroom and a family space out of the living room. The sculpture and graphics are by Kari Huhtamo.

FRESH PERSPECTIVE ON A MODERN MIX

Ristomatti Ratia's Helsinki home reflects the international character of its owner's lifestyle. It is open and breezy—easy to live in when he is there and simple to put in order when he returns from traveling. Lots of fresh flowers, all-of-a-kind in a pot, add small masses of color and life to white-white walls and floors with trim of stripped pine. Original doors, a few blond antiques and a big Italian market umbrella set off mostly modern furnishings. As creative head of Marimekko, Ratia wants from his home what he does of his

other creations—that they be all at once "architectural, romantic, colorful… and sometimes black and white."

His is one of the charmingly railroaded flats in a National Romantic style building in a quarter of the city that is nearly homogenous in its turn-of-the-century look. The modern approach to its interior design is as open as the plan that offers a strong axial view of rooms framed by the openings of other rooms. All the heavy old doors were left in place with the intention of playing

Every room in this see-through apartment has two or three doorways that open onto adjoining spaces. Stripped pine doors frame the views; glossy white floors give continuity with polish. Here, the living room , left, and the bedroom seen past the dining room's market umbrella and tile stove.

up that vista while cutting into its field of vision with smaller, textural planes that can be angled at will. The whiteness of the space and the clean lines of its unmatched furniture provide a background for art and changing still-life treatments of favorite objects. Old toy horses balance contemporary graphics and strong furniture in soft hues. Bouquets of lush summer flowers add gentleness against an abstract painting or cool marble tabletop.

One has the feeling that the rooms could be nearly interchangeable except for the areas that are deliberately built-in. At one end of the apartment is a kitchen blessed with all the natural light a bay of three windows can provide, employing an unusual hexagonal counter arrangement, to take full advantage of the room's interesting shape. At the other end is a built-in sleeping platform with storage and headboard of light weight design that nearly disappears into the space. Over rooftops are uninterrupted views letting in the sky and a quality of light that continually changes.

An antique rocking horse in the modern environment is a Ratia trademark. His plan makes full use of the irregular kitchen space.

Flowers fresh from an outdoor marketplace sit in a repainted wooden office chair. Ratia's half-sphere opal vase design accessorizes the all-white dining space.

The hallway, with antique pine cabinets and table, leads to the kitchen. A living-room corner is treated minimally with Italian furniture and a painting by Tapies.

2
OUTSIDE

EXTERIOR VIEW

Face to face with a Finnish house, one still senses the sky, land, sea. In a country known for its architecture, this is a tribute to the success of the manmade and a sign of the link between form and materials that keeps shapes square and low, and unifies the look of old and new homes. Everywhere the box-shaped house dots the countryside—the oldest are likely to be of hand-hewn logs with neatly interlocking corner joints, the newest might be of prefabricated steel and wood panels carefully constructed to assemble quickly and true.

Nature has been both the donor and beneficiary of such design. She has always supplied the primary material—wood—and through the ages has challenged primitive hunters and modern engineers alike to build up to her demanding standards. Techniques have endured that weather well: pitched roofs supported by heavy beams, eaves and overhangs of generous scale, earthy stains and paints that protect as they add cheer. Days of intensive sun or darkness, moist springs and frozen winters—extremes are the norm. Paying attention has meant not only survival but alliance. In heeding nature's ways, Finns have formed a close bond with their surroundings; as in many relationships, struggle has led to respect. People are careful to build solidly but tread lightly in nature when constructing a house. Habit honors the coastline and forest; building laws ensure their integrity today.

In cities too, the natural environment is a presence. Town plans that grew and changed over the years, spilling over onto coastal islands, continue to incorporate parks, beaches and walkways by the water's edge. Systems of broad streets and low buildings keep the sky open and the manmade scale human. Practical considerations at first dictated such plans: fires had wiped out whole neighborhoods of wooden houses before early-nineteenth-century architects proposed a grid plan of wide avenues and low detached houses to prevent the spread of flames. The formality of that neoclassical arrangement gives a tidy look to the blocks of dwellings with wide low-pitched roofs, board and batten facades and simple trim that remain from that period. Such a plan turned city blocks of houses inward; while they presented their consistent low-relief surfaces to the street, small pleasant courtyards walled-off by slat fences bloomed within.

Meanwhile, in the countryside, peasant houses and farms were built in the same dark timber styles as they had been for centuries with outbuildings forming a kind of irregular courtyard in front of the main house. At more prosperous farms, plans ranged from close scatterings of more than a dozen small barns and work houses to long groupings of joined shelters that formed an enclosed protective court. Households grew as children took spouses or unmarried brothers and sisters stayed on, or as hired hands were engaged. Separate outbuildings were constructed each with a quite specific farm activity in mind and were freely added when domestic storage was required. Some storehouses had lofts that were used as summer sleeping and sitting rooms by extended family members and especially by young people of courting age. Varied techniques for fashioning balconies, doors, overhangs and corner joints give strong, simple character and charm to these small weather-beaten or earth-stained structures.

As buildings changed character in outlying areas with growing sophistication and passing styles, houses that had been made from logs squared off by hand gave way to those of logs veneered in sawn planks for more insulation; they were easier to paint and make fancy with detail. Neoclassical touches found appreciation here too as pleasing symmetry enhanced straightforward home design and logical Empire detailing seemed an elegant way to finish joints. Thus, pilasters could conveniently cover the log ends of interior walls where they jutted out, carpenters' pediments would decorate and protect seams above windows. Such ornamentation was applied with a restraint befitting people whose eye was sharpened by a taste for the plain and whose preference for economy of line was moulded by the economics of a rugged life.

Later, National Romantic and Art Nouveau styles were interpreted in a similar way in houses of outlying areas, by adding door frames and window or roof trim consistent with those looks to the same boxy wooden body. However, these last styles made their strongest impact on emerging neighborhoods in cities at a time when they were rapidly growing at the dawn of the twentieth century. Whole schemes were developed for areas of apartment houses and fine private dwellings. Decorative details ranged from picturesque imagery of berry bush and elk interpreted in heavy granite or solid wood with ironwork trim, to the more Continental motifs that lyrically integrated turrets and balconies into pastel-hued smooth stucco facades.

By the 1930s, increasingly cleaned-up classical facades—a reaction against decorative treatments from the turn of the century—were being supplanted by the first buildings in the functionalist style and Finland's own endorsement of Bauhaus principles began to take shape. The shape new homes took was simple. The square dwelling, historically efficient to heat with its central stove and easiest to construct from heavy timber, now became expressive in form of the minimal modern esthetic. Technology made it possible to open up interior space according to comfort and use, provided options in materials and new support systems, and eventually made it possible to produce standardized building components. Contemporary taste had much in common with country traditions, and the simple shape that hugged the horizon found new favor. Even as apartment buildings were planned, multiples of the square module were employed in their scaling in an attempt to ensure proportions that were contextually coherent. The discipline for thinking clean and clutter-free had been handed down. Craftsman-like pride in handling materials and engineering-like insistence on solutions that worked created a new high standard of housing for all.

A COURTYARD WITH A DIFFERENCE

This is a three o'clock house," says architect Elissa Aalto of her home in the country designed by her husband and completed in 1952. Indeed, the courtyard garden, the most intriguing part of the building, requires strong summer light to be seen at its best. It is the way the sun throws the extraordinary brickwork into relief that makes it come alive.

Alvar Aalto used this house to experiment with that material and, to a lesser extent, with glazed tile during a period in which he was using them often in his work. Some sections of the courtyard walls here at Muuratsalo serve as models for techniques used in the next few years for the House of Culture and Pensions Institute projects in Helsinki. For their home, Aalto created a patchwork effect that gives a gay appearance to serious, personal architecture.

Courtyards belong to some of the oldest Finnish houses—rural homes made use of flanking outbuildings to create that space in front; in cities, courts were behind the main house. Aalto had developed the courtyard idea in plans since the 1920s: Villa Mairea's L-shape takes

advantage of such a space for a private relaxation area; his own studio in Helsinki incorporates a terraced amphitheatre-like court. Mrs. Aalto notes that they had recently traveled to Rome before this house was planned. Fresh impressions of the classical atrium may well have reinforced his belief in the sheltered garden as part of the ideal plan for a house.

Here, the wedge-shaped structure—another characteristic Aalto motif—is oriented south toward the long view down the lake and the warmest rays of the sun. The atrium walls frame both the lake and the house in pleasing ways. Like a ruin, the open court invites the eye to fill in gaps, to play on textured surfaces. Chaise longues are arranged casually; wild strawberries grow by the door.

The house is approached on a path through the trees; its white facade sits low to the ground. The surprise is in walking around to the side and encountering the lifting form that breaks to reveal its heart of red brick. Above, the "fractured" west wall onto which Aalto introduced heavy climbing vines.

From remote farms in Lapland to new apartments facing the Helsinki harbor, the box-shaped Finnish form is ubiquitous. An affinity for right angles and low cubic volumes seems to organize the appearance of barns and scattered houses in the countryside, wooden side-by-side townhouses with neoclassical detailing, turn-of-the-century apartment buildings and even contemporary prefabricated wood and steel garden apartments, painted traditionally in red and black.

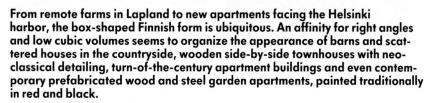

Turn-of-the-century towers for city dwellings are interpreted in the more massive National Romantic and lighter Art Nouveau styles. This deliberate borrowing of themes from antiquity and nature, and recombining them with forms from the Finnish vernacular is not unlike the kind of post-modern experimentation that is undertaken today in other parts of the world.

148

The pastel-hued exteriors from the early 1800s and those influenced by the Continental Art Nouveau that were constructed in the first years of this century are romantic surprises in this northern locale. At left and top, are buildings with classical detailing on Suomenlinna, the cluster of old fortress islands at the mouth of Helsinki harbor. Today, several of the structures, commissioned by the Czar as military housing, have been renovated as apartments. Below, in a residential neighborhood of the city, is an apartment building in the Art Nouveau style, in Finland referred to as *Jugend* because of its closer resemblance to the German architecture of the period than the French.

A range of exterior window treatments on wood and stucco facades of houses from various periods: simple crossed boards, restrained interpretations of neo-classical and rococo styles, decorative *Jugend* details, highly ornamental late 19th-century carpenters' creations, and straightforward modern shapes. Moss is still sometimes used on windowsills as a charming means of blocking drafts (at right).

Warm welcomes are given by a host of doorways with pleasing propor-tions...rural slatted types to which paint gives simple distinction, care-fully mitred heavy herringbone patterns, fanciful 19th-century wood relief work and canopies of metal, bold National Romantic statements in granite that frame carved panels with iron trim. By the stoop is often a small twig broom for whisking shoes before entering; a country custom is to lay pine branches before the sill for a scent-releasing scrape of the feet.

FORESTS, FIELDS & FLOWERS

In Finland the countryside is never far away. Flat plains, calm lakes, silent mossy forests and a vast archipelago give great tranquility to the natural landscape. The sky looks bigger, the trees appear straighter than elsewhere; the sea seems to be everywhere. Once it nearly was. Most of southern and central Finland was covered by the Baltic Sea until some eight thousand years ago. A rise in the land created the lake district and brought the south coast and islands above sea level. That process continues today at a slower pace, giving another ten square kilometers every year to the maritime towns and fishing villages on the gulfs of the Baltic that wrap around the country. Finland's is a shy loveliness, not a showy beauty. Everything seems to have its place in such a setting, including man.

Here the horizon has strength. Unobstructed vistas draw the shimmer of water into view from great distances and quietly call attention to the unassuming volumes of scattered farmhouses, barns, a church. A sense of distance develops perspective; Finns are far-sighted about nature. The Lapps who live above the arctic circle, historically a nomadic people, like to speak of their culture as one that shows its sophistication through an ability to live in harmony with the environment for thousands of years without leaving traces. The kinship all Finns feel with their surroundings leaves them less inclined to disturb nature, more interested in appreciating it as it is.

Outdoors, a less-is-more philosophy means framing the landscape in pleasing ways, creating places to enjoy the view, rather than altering the terrain or planting gardens judged grand by European or American defini-tion. Gazebos are built on gentle hills or atop mounds of granite. A footpath or simple boardwalk leads through forest and field to a log bench at water's edge. Saunas are erected by lake or seaside for cleansing dips but also to offer a peaceful view across the water during rest-time after bathing. Often wildflowers and groves of slender trees are integrated into the grounds of a house. Allées of lilac or birch might be planted along a drive or pathway. Flowers are likely to follow the lines of rock or timber foundations of the oldest houses, gayly softening their solidity. In contemporary homes too, plantings may bloom by gatepost and fence or at the base of a tree rather than in a formalized garden. In towns, small inner courtyards offer pos-sibilities for punctuating facades, cellars or outcroppings of rock with splashes of living color.

Summer owes its intensity to the gift of sun after many dark months: birds sing almost constantly, pausing only at noon and during the few twi-light hours around midnight in the south; pale, small-leafed birches and lilacs in tones from pink and mauve to purple burst forth; wild berries flower and ripen to a sweetness unmatched by cultivated types. Autumn is a golden time spotted with red bushes and berries and hundreds of mush-room varieties, some colorful enough to compete in beauty with the late-summer flowers of other climes. The subtlety of winter brings another palette: lakes and sea freeze silvery solid; a blanket of snow whitens the land from around Christmas to Easter and makes dark days reflect back lighter; pine, fir and spruce show deep green through somber whites and grays.

156

The calm of the natural landscape becomes a source of personal pleasure. Overlooks and walkways bring the quiet beauty into focus.

PLAYING THE ROMANTIC

A garden by the sea draws on the slope and small inlets for inspiration in plantings and pathways. Indigenous sea grasses and lily pads are framed by willows; ferns and soft hedges fill in around gates and lawn furniture. A series of small bridges are for fancy...they play on perspective, leading nowhere.

Fresh, white-painted furniture of all types is set about the grassy greens. Aino Aalto's garden-swing design is seen at top.

PLEASURE IN THE BALANCE

A classical approach to house and garden creates the satisfying symmetry of the grounds plan for a southwestern manor. Gravel walks, centered fountain and sundial are simply articulated, and carefully placed. A lilac allée leads to the sea and affords a glimpse of the water from the rear veranda.

An 18th-century manor house sits on land originally awarded the family by the King of Sweden in 1654. Classical details show in pediments, columns and veranda balustrade.

The front porch and side wings are early-19th-century additions
to the house built in 1763, and are thought to be designed by an important
neo-classical architect of that time, C. F. Bassi. An Italian by birth, he became
Finland's first controller of public works. Climbing vines cool the cream-
colored porch and its painted furniture made by a regional carpenter. The
faceted columns and weathered paints draw attention to the linear aspect
of the woodwork.

Furniture made locally is a country interpretation of classical and Art Nouveau styles.

Gazebos and garden pavilions provide idyllic panoramas of the sea, treetops or green meadows. Such are the settings of late sunlit summer dinners or autumn crayfish parties. Divergent styles find expression in wood here, too, from carpenters' gothic to National Romantic.

166

Modest courts and small yards yield colorful contrasts and ingenious garden ideas: twig hoops to edge a circular bed, open-work planter box contained by sod, birdhouses integrated into birch groves or bright ground cover, a water trough made of wood staves hooped with split branches.

Silent, snow-laden pines form
receding planes of light and dark.
Forests cover more than two-thirds
of the land here.

Seasonal extremes explain clever ways with lighting. The darkest days culminate in candlelit Christmas. Here, ice lanterns were made for planting in the snow or illuminating walkways. To make them, water is allowed to stand overnight in buckets; it freezes first at the sides and on top. When it is dumped out and reversed, the hollow is perfect for a column candle.

Outdoor decorations enliven winter's monotone. A range of wreaths are shaped from evergreens and, at top, from the pale puffs of moss that nourish reindeer. The simplest birdfeeder is made by hanging sheaves of oats on a tree or fence; birds perch on the stalks and peck at grains. Here, oats are hung by a rustic log birdhouse.

173

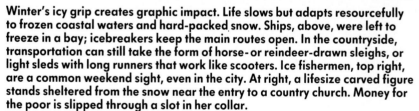

Winter's icy grip creates graphic impact. Life slows but adapts resourcefully to frozen coastal waters and hard-packed snow. Ships, above, were left to freeze in a bay; icebreakers keep the main routes open. In the countryside, transportation can still take the form of horse- or reindeer-drawn sleighs, or light sleds with long runners that work like scooters. Ice fishermen, top right, are a common weekend sight, even in the city. At right, a lifesize carved figure stands sheltered from the snow near the entry to a country church. Money for the poor is slipped through a slot in her collar.

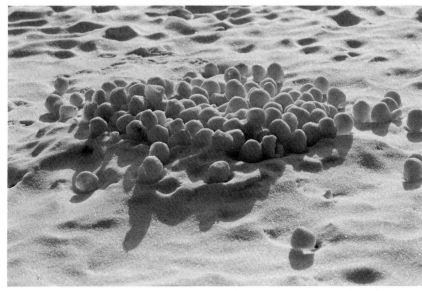

MIDSUMMER

The magic of primeval Finland is now conjured up but once a year, on Midsummer night. The celebration of the summer solstice is an ancient pagan ritual, but the miracle of the white Nordic night seems no less worth rejoicing in today. After the long winter—with darkness that lasts 1½ months in the far north, broken only by the great silent waves of northern lights that glow in the inky sky—the coming of the sweet greens and lilac-scented early summer is a seductive happening. The midnight sun of Lapland, and twenty-hour daylight in the summer of the south, change the pace of life for man as for nature. Midsummer marks the beginning of warmth and fulsome growth. Days stretch out and slow down, long light evenings are a gift of time.

Midsummer has always been a day to make merry with family and friends. Historically, whole villages gathered together to light a bonfire and dance around it until the new day dawned. The light of these great pyres, sometimes thirty feet in height, reflected all along the southern coast and through the chains of inland lakes, as people gazed into them for signs of good fortune and a bountiful summer ahead. Music played all night from a small hand-held harp, magic words were chanted, wreaths were brought to the festivities, woven of field flowers. On the west coast and in the offshore islands, fishermen and their families made tall mast-like poles and deco-

Midsummer is celebrated with bonfires or by erecting tall poles strung with greenery and carvings. Wildflower bouquets and birch branches adorn homes and boats.

rated them with leaves and wildflowers strung up in hourglass shapes, and topped them with whittled sailboats and the likeness of a villager.

The coming of the fertile season was a time for thoughts of love. Traditions varied, but spells were always cast with the hope of finding happiness and inspiring one's true love. Sometimes a young maiden was to bathe naked in the dew of the field of her beloved, planting within him the wish to marry her. Or she might sprinkle flowers into the spring as a love offering, when she fetched the water for her evening's bathing. She could make her bath whisk from nine different birch trees growing at a crossroads or weave together a special whisk from only yellow flowers.

Today, the romance lingers. The full blossoming of nature is cause for festivities that commence with the rite of sauna and last late into the blue-white night round a tall fire. Birch branches are cut and brought up to the house to frame its doorways and decorate every room, as symbols of good luck. It is the day for big dinners, for many toasts, for making the nightless night last longer. It is the time for making the freshest *vihtas*, birch bath whisks, and for storing them away until the days when trees are bare. Wreaths are worn in the hair or hung about the house. Bunches of lilacs and daisies and bachelor buttons are gathered, but the nicest bouquets continue to be those of sweet clover, soft grasses and mixed flowers of the field.

Bonfires glow along the coast on the nightless night.

All-night celebrations are illuminated by candles outside and in. A recycled dairy barn, at left, serves for a Midsummer party with young birch branches wrapping the posts and candles floating in the water trough.

COUNTRY COTTAGES

Every summer Finland seems to go back about one hundred years in time. The cities empty out, the population returns to the soil—to the fertile river valleys of the west or the wooded peninsulas of the lake district or the scrub-covered fells of the north or the rocky shores of the archipelago or the grassy meadows of the coast. Among bankers as among boatmen, the instinct to return to the country during the much-cherished green months pulls people away from twentieth-century conveniences and resettles them in more primitive dwellings reminiscent of simpler days. Everyone who can chooses to resume the rhythm of life at its most basic, in harmony with the wind and water and woods.

A land of sixty thousand lakes and thirty thousand coastal islands whose soil is largely covered by pine, birch, and spruce forests, unspoiled Finland lures even country people into a plainer existence. Some people have a small island to call their own, reachable only by boat except when the lakes and sea freeze over in winter and one can ski or drive there on ice. Another may retreat to a homemade cabin, hiking in to a wooded knoll where no roads go. Or one might pitch a tent in a field or breezy barn no longer in use. In every case, a country place offers more rustic shelter and an earthier existence. It reorders the routines of living, putting one in touch with the outdoors anew.

For country cottages, the rule of thumb is the simpler, the more dear. Often without indoor plumbing or central heating, the houses rely on sauna and wood stove to serve as ever. A sauna can even do for living a week or so at a time, its benches fit for sleeping with bedrolls as in the tradition of the *tupa,* its fireplace giving heat or flames to cook by, its changing room acting as a place to sit and to eat. Going to one's summer house means getting away from it all, not just from the workplace and pace of modern life, but from neighbors too. It is a way of celebrating solitude for the descendents of hunters, fishermen and farmers. The custom of displacing oneself come summer is as old as some of the old farmsteads. Children, in-laws and hired hands moved into the unheated loft rooms in barns then for seasonal house-keeping and also in deference to each person's due privacy. And cooking sometimes shifted to outdoor ovens protected by pole-tent arrangements. By the late nineteenth century, a growing middle class was beginning to adapt to the new notion of "vacation"—but not as in the grand seaside hotels along the promenades of southern European coasts. Instead, one took a simple rural cabin that represented, as it does now, not only a change in locale but a shift in way of life.

Writer Agnes Rothery described Finnish summer-home life this way after her journey through the archipelago in 1936: "To own an island the size of a crumb, clap on it a house the size of a fly-speck and a bath house the size of a gnat-speck with a boat and a flag pole and, of course, a Finnish flag! And there you are…in an amber of crystal air and crystal sea, suspended for three months…between the sky and the water."

TO SIT
BY THE SEA

First find the safe harbor for the boat, then build the house nearby—this is the philosophy of the fishermen who live on these islands," says Heikki Siren, "and it is still the best approach." He and his wife created

A stark shape in weathered wood, "Kappeli" is temple-like. Here, the Finns' kinship with the Japanese in their relationship to nature is apparent. The structure sits on piled rocks with dead airspace underneath.

185

a system of piled rocks and interconnected floats to dock their boat, then built the sauna and sleeping areas. Next, a place to cook and sit around a table was added. Much later came "Kappeli," a kind of free space on the highest point of rock.

The "Chapel," as they have nicknamed it, is a rustic extravagance that gives shelter to the wish to be part of the glittering open sea, the pounding

of a summer storm, the stillness of a moonlit evening. This is the other side of the island from the harbor, the one that takes the severest beatings of a changeable climate. When winds are heavy, wooden braces are brought in to secure the glass walls.

The surprise of "Kappeli" is in traversing wooden plankways from the cove side, through a cool glade where ferns and blueberries grow, to

emerge on sheer rock with its simple shrine of a structure now weathered as gray as the granite all around it. The room took its proportions from the rocks but, like them, loses all scale when you look back at it from a distance. Low benches with linen covers are its only adornment except for collected stones. Straight lines satisfy in such surroundings where one confronts the quiet strength of the horizon. Woods and coastline supply soothing curves.

Four tree trunks support the building. In a turn-around from tradition, vertical rather than horizontal members carry the weight. Lines are straight and clean; only the circular front step and roll-back of the seating repeat the rounded form of the trunk posts. Cushions conceal built-in storage underneath the hinged seat platforms.

SIMPLE PARADISE
IN PINE

The cabin sits in a conifer forest. Inside, the continuity of log surfaces is broken only by a stone chimney and soft materials that add warmth: generous cotton pillows on the banquette, sheepskins and *ryijy* rug, the woolly man-made replacement for animal furs.

A one-room cabin in the woods furnishes nothing in the way of con-veniences and everything in terms of escape. Outside a village in Lapland, nestled down a dirt road that leads to a foot path, it is hard to find even when you are searching for it. This is a forest of reindeer roundups, where the otherwise freely grazing animals are corraled temporarily and marked in autumn. Its cushion of green moss provides nourishment for the deer

(who know to dig down for it through the snow) and turns purple-red in fall with lingonberries and heather.

The rustic look of hefty one-log-thick walls dominates outside and inside. Practical furniture is made from more of the same. A wall-to-wall banquette filled with jumbo, black canvas pillows spans one side of the room. Stubby log stools pull up to the fire. Benches and table are of smoothed split logs. Local rocks were used to build a chimney that draws from two fireplaces, one on the seating side, another in a cooking corner. Post and lintel arrangement support a stepped mantel where lots of votive candles always flicker against steel-gray stone. At each end of the cabin an open loft furnishes overhead mattress space. Spillover guests can bed down on the banquette below.

IN A CLUSTER OF CABINS

Here on a pencil-point peninsula, formed in the retreat of the Ice Age glacier, it is possible in the summer months to see the sun rising even as it is setting. This is one of three parallel narrow strips of land that jut way out into a lake thirteen kilometers long in central Finland. A cluster arrangement of wooden cabins make up a seasonal retreat so far— in state of mind as

in distance—that it can only be reached by motor boat in calm weather, by skis over the frozen lake in winter, or by horseback through the forest anytime. The Periäinen family use all three means. The midsummer hush surrounding the small buildings that stand teepee-like in the birches keeps a secret of the tribal disputes over fishing waters and hunting rights along

Black-stained walls and tar-paper roofs camouflage the units in the forest's shadow. Log foundations level the structures in pine needles and grass. A deck that projects from the living-room cabin offers a lake view.

The *tupa* hut has cast-iron stove, banquettes that convert for sleeping and games table. In the tidy kitchen, a central stove is the pivotal point around which storage and seating are built-in; gear hangs on a branch above. The symmetrical sleeping cabin for two daughters is at right.

this ancient territorial boundary. Locals still refer to the three penisulas as Point of the Petty Thief, Point of Verdict and Point of the Tombs, according to the tales of those times.

Mr. Periäinen, an architect, conceived of the unique living arrangement as a result of the land's shape and as a way to give personal freedom to all family members. The ease with which one can slip away for a summer read

or nap justifies his efforts. Further, all appreciate the way the separate cabins force them to go outside in all kinds of weather; the children point out that otherwise they might have missed one of the displays of northern lights in winter or the moose that swam over in summer. The weather-proofed structures sit up off the earth on massive crossed logs, a traditional method of keeping out dampness and small animals. The dark stain was chosen because it causes the houses to fall into shadow, so they are hardly noticed until just before landing by boat. Four small buildings make up the grouping—living room, kitchen/sauna, plus two sleeping units. The former two are insulated so only those are used when the family skis over for a week's stay in winter; long benches in both quickly convert to sleeping places. Beds and seating are mostly built-in providing lots of storage under hinged platforms.

GOING THE SIMPLEST ROUTE

Tenting in an old grain barn seems the most unencumbered way to get access to the country for Yrjö and Kristina Wiherheimo. Kristina, born in Lapland, shares a love for the wilderness with her architect-husband. The two spend as much vacation time as possible in the far north; going year-round to the Arctic Ocean where they keep an old steam-powered fishing boat. The barn they like to camp in sits in a pasture near the arctic circle, moved there by friends whose house is nearby. Even when the barn was "new" its logs were recycled from other outbuildings, giving them a built-life of many hundred years. Yet their condition is still sound owing to good joints and the venting effect of centuries-old off-the-ground building methods. Mrs. Wiherheimo, an artist, handprinted the cotton and sewed the tent. The idea of pitching it indoors is an old country custom—a way to mosquito-proof an airy *aitta* for summer sleeping. Here, rag runners play one of their historic roles, as bedcovers.

The old grain barn was repainted in its original colors. Its raised foundation balances over buttercups on four rocks; a log fitted with treads leads to the door. A corner ladder gives access to the loft where the tent is pitched.

FARM STRATEGY FOR A SUMMER PLACE

We wanted a house we could pound a nail into without worry when we want to hang something," architect Matti Vuorio explains. "The surfaces are intentionally somewhat rough." He, his architect-wife and children come to their weekend place year-round to relax and to work. The property on which the house sits, four hectares of fields and one of forest, helps to support their pleasure. A yearly harvest of three thousand kilos of potatoes

and Jersualem artichokes goes to market, to friends, to their own root cellar for the winter, and comes in handy as a gift to a country doctor or neighbors who refuse to accept payment for their help.

The Vuorios worked out their own system for affording a country house at a time when their own design practice was young and might not otherwise have sustained it. They bought in farm country, rather than at the shore

The simple shape of the house is given more depth by posts and beams, left to weather naturally, that support the structure and frame the porches. Concrete well components are cut and stacked to form an outdoor grill. Down the slope, the pool is carefully terraced so as not to disrupt the view.

where land is about twice as expensive and chose to help finance their weekend life with the resources of the land, as any rural family would. They used plain materials and worked with them ingeniously to create open shelves, hanging systems, curtain-fronted closets, benches, beds, even an outdoor grill. They invested their own labor when feasible and built as big as they could afford at the time, netting a house they will not outgrow.

A well-thought-out energy plan contributes to their comfort and makes certain luxuries possible. Says Vuorio, "Sauna is the core." When they arrive in chilly weather, the first fire is built there. It warms up the seating area above too, a place where everyone has learned to congregate. In all but the warmest months, they take advantage of a government incentive to encourage an equal time spread of energy draw, buying their electric heat at night at half the daytime rate. A coil system starts the heat circulating under the tiled main floor at ten o'clock each evening; the tiles store and radiate heat through the next day. Centralized fireplaces and a wood-fueled kitchen stove act as back-ups. A solar collector heats a spring-fed pool to a comfortable swimming temperature in just one day.

Outdoor spaces expand the modest house; an upstairs porch has climbing ropes for kids and a "wall" of dried birch branches left from sauna use; a sheltered porch acts as a mudroom; and a root cellar holds potato and Jerusalem artichoke crops. Life centers inside around the open kitchen and the den hearth built above the sauna.

OPEN AIR PAVILION

A summer house that reads like an airy cubistic pavilion is the home of architect Ilkka Salo and his wife Laura. "The idea was to create something that lays gently in the grass like a bird's egg," says Salo, "where the hard forms of wood stand in contrast to the soft natural greens." Placed in a grove of birch and aspen, whose floor blooms white and fragrant with lily of the valley in spring, the house is opaque and sculptural from one side, translucent on the other. Grayed wood walls provide privacy and insulation on the north, glass walls shaded by blinds face a quiet bay on the south. The center is pierced by a pair of decks.

The use of space is as free as the rooms and decks are open. The two rooms both have sitting and sleeping areas; one includes a pullman kitchen, the other a table for drawing or dining. The Salos use the room whose wall slides away, opening onto nature and giving them a feeling of sleeping outdoors. Full curtains soften the door frames of both. The decks become outdoor rooms as the weather allows, when furniture shifts according to need and parachute cloth may be laid over beams to shade fresh-air dining. The simplest furnishings and all-weather surfaces foster an attitude of laissez-faire summertime living.

200

Indoor and outdoor spaces connect effortlessly with pocket doors and others of glass that swing wide. A small sauna sits across the deck from the bedroom. Nature comes up to the decks on both sides.

A view of the house through high birches in front; an undisturbed
view out to sea past calm coastal sea grass in back.

ISLAND ESCAPE

A fisherman's cottage built in 1964 became a getaway in the archipelago for a family from Turku, the former capital of Finland and gateway to the islands. A simple wood structure that provided shelter was improved, and additions were made over the last ten years so that the whole now consists of two main log buildings joined by a deck, and an old *savusauna* that sits in a grassy cove. A deep, warm oxblood stain penetrates and

protects exteriors; precision joinery ensures their tightness. Arrival on this tiny island is by seaplane or boat. It is one of hundreds of islands inhabited among thousands in the chain between Finland and Sweden where the climate can be kinder because of its southwestern locale, but where winds are wicked at times and changes in weather unpredictable.

The house sits low on the spot where granite meets meadow, with its

Island living gives both isolation and openness. Unobtrusive cottages on next islands share the same advantages. The main deck is a summer living room; white wood furniture was designed by Aino Aalto in 1939.

large windows and deck giving a splendid view of the open sea and the nearest neighbor islands that bob, just barely visible, on the horizon. The materials for the addition were sent down the coast by boat from interior forests where trees had been hand-picked for the job. A craftsman—fittingly named Cricket—chose the trees, cut them to fit, laid them together in mock assembly, took them apart and had them loaded on the boat, then saw to the on-island building. Measurements can only be done once for such a project and must guarantee perfect fit; knowledge of the wood's properties

in a humid environment is all-important. The sleekness and simplicity of its final appearance make the place as deliberately understated from a distance as was the original cottage in the days when sheep grazed these grasses in a rotational farm system common to the archipelago. Life here depends on each day's weather. The morning's catch could be that night's dinner; bottled water is fetched from the mainland when the sea permits, as with other provisions. Cleverly simple systems enhance the enjoyment: rain barrels catch wash water, gas lamps and candles give the only light.

The efficiency of these small rooms seems to expand the space; kitchen and living-room design are by Pirkko Stenros. Ingenious ideas make the simple life pleasant: floating candles and flowers for night-lighting on a porch; washing with crushed ferns and rain water; warming dinner plates on the stone hearth. Glassed-in porch and decks connect the rooms.

SAUNA

Some say the pleasure of sauna begins in chopping wood to make the fire or in gathering the leafy, fragrant birch branches from the edge of the forest to bind into bath whisks, in anticipation of the ancient Finnish ritual. A way of bathing that dates back thousands of years to a time when sophisticated Europeans were more prone to douse themselves with perfume than with water, sauna has little to do with the daily shower most of us pop in and out of today. It is both the time sauna takes and the timelessness of the ritual that makes it appealing. For a Finn, it is as common as a cup of coffee and as special as a holiday feast. Sauna is an everyday event for some—for country people during harvest and haymaking, and for anybody who simply prefers sweating it out to standing under a faucet— an end-of-the-week treat for most and a celebration at festival times for everyone. Sauna is both a holy ceremony and a way to entertain friends on Saturday night.

Sauna is sensual and yet its propriety in Finland might be compared to the tea ceremony in Japan. Families sit quietly in the wooden chamber following the steps of sauna together. To invite guests is to extend a politeness expressing the wish to share the intimacy and pleasure of the experience. The host will make the sauna ready: prepare the stove, pour warmed water into wooden buckets for washing, lay out towels, ladle water on the heated rocks to produce a cloud of steam when the dry heat needs moisture, and quite unselfconsciously offer to flick the visitor's moist and reddened skin with a leafy birch bundle, or *vihta*, to stimulate circulation. He may also offer a scrubbing with pine soap and a soft root brush or a vigorous rub with a linen towel. It is hard to feel distant from one who scrubs your back so well. In pagan times sauna was connected with special powers and the spirit of the gods. Its magic is no less potent now. One emerges from the wonderful torture of repeated heatings and coolings feeling thoroughly cleansed and spiritually revived.

There is one sauna for about every four people in Finland. They are standard in apartment houses, dormitories and hotels, and a familiar sight in any private home. But the best are the wooden huts of the countryside that are situated away from the main house and down near the lake or sea, offering up their sense of physical refreshment and emotional well-being from within a surround of heavy but softly radiant logs, tucked in a thicket of trees and bushes. The sauna should sit a walk away from the water for a brisk plunge or quick slip through a hole in the ice after bathing in the heat, yet not disturb the look of the coastline for others. The outer room will face west if possible to give a glimpse of the last rays of sun in the restful afterglow of bathing.

The oldest sauna was a kind of underground dugout; about two thousand years ago this was improved by constructing a timber cabin with overlapping joints and birchbark or turf roof to house the fireplace of piled rocks, crude benches and barrels of water. Since that time saunas have been modernized—they are available in prefab components that can be dropped into minimal square footage in any new apartment—but they have never been improved. There is a gentleness about the chimneyless *savusauna*, the old smoke sauna, that comes from hours of preparatory stoking and firing the rocks until their centers are red hot and the embers have died down, the pungent smoky smell given off by the blackened interior timbers after years of heatings, the unnoticed movement of air through tiny chinks in the logs and small square openings carved out as vents low in its walls. It is always dusk inside, for these slats offer the only light until after sunset when a candle may illuminate the space.

There is a deep, dark beauty about this primitive shelter that is enriched by understanding its place in Finnish homelife since earliest times —as the room where babies were born (with heat and access, to water, it was most hygienic), the place for ministering the sick, the first living quarters while the main house and farm were being built, the laundry and workplace for beating and drying harvested flax, the smokehouse for meat, the drying hut for grain…in addition, of course, to its primary role as bath house. Even in the early years of the twentieth century it was said that one who entered the world through sauna entered most safely.

A HANDHEWN HUT

Anew *savusauna* was designed and made in the customary way by workmen from Lapland who know the art of building with kelo logs cut from trees that die and harden while standing. Its forthright chunky shape echoes the solidity and warmth it offers. Rounded rocks from the sea bottom were gathered to make its stove; tapping them for the right pitch is one way to know that those chosen are hard enough to withstand hours of high heat. In keeping with the tradition of the smoke sauna, all furniture and accessories here were simply fashioned from local pine and birch—bench, stool, table, hollowed-out soap dish and birchbark basket.

There is a small entry for removing clothing and a front porch with rustic furniture for sitting or taking the air between heatings. Water buckets in the heat room are blackened, like the walls, by the smoke.

ALL THAT SAUNA HAS TO OFFER

Anew sauna made from old materials reflects a young architect's appreciation for tradition. Georg Grotenfelt recycled heavy logs from the walls of an old barn and built new fittings with natural, light pine to contrast with and lighten the weightiness of the old. The solution is not only an esthetic one, it is his way of helping to redress the abandonment of beautiful old farm buildings in the wake of Finland's postwar shift from agrarian to urban society. The light vertical members also break into and warm up large expanses of glass in the sauna's outer room, used for changing and for resting afterwards. All the freestanding benches of his design can be moved around as one wishes—ganged as a place to lie down, or brought outside as a way to take the air.

Although modeled on the layout of sauna typical to Savo in

Heating and washing take place in the same room in this sauna; the slope of the roof helps the hot air to rise up to the platform of benches. Their U-formation, with bathers seated upright facing each other, is typical of eastern Finland. Well-located window slits reflect sun off the lake throwing soft light against interior surfaces. Both the changing room and porch can be used for after-sauna relaxation, depending on the season.

eastern Finland, in the largest sense this is representative of all that sauna has to offer. It was the architect's intention to open as many options as possible to its users, within the boundaries of sauna tradition. His choices are symbolic as well as pleasing to eye and body. Logs stacked under a back overhang first meet your glance on the way down the pine-needle path to the cabin. "Without wood there would not be sauna," suggests Grotenfelt, who has routed the walk thusly. Next, a chimney catches your attention, a clear red symbol of the energy fired by wood. Glass walls on the lakeside invite the natural environment up to the building. A turf roof keeps the hut well-integrated in the green landscape, helps insulate in winter, and hints that sauna, like those who use it, belong to the earth.

213

The changing room is a glass enclosure attached to the log walls of the heating/washing room. Its new form and materials were planned to contrast with the old. Though rather close to the lake, the sauna disappears nicely in the grass and trees.

215

BOATHOUSE TO SAUNA

A boathouse at the end of a dock was converted by dividing the interior into three rooms: heat room, wash room and a generous sitting room with table, benches and canvas swing. A dock extension with a ladder into the sea at its open end allows one to take the plunge directly from shelter.

Here, the sauna is seen at Midsummer. A float of birches will be pulled out to sea and lit as a bonfire at twilight. Birch branches are used inside as festive decoration.

WINTER WARMTH

In this sauna, one undresses on the porch. The simple, one-room interior is stoked up for a hot bath on the banks of the icy lake.

A classic one-room smoke sauna sits by a frozen lake. Smoke curls up from the chimney all afternoon; the fire is lit hours ahead in the piled rock fireplace. As the heat builds, inside temperatures can reach 200°C (390°F). Before bathing, the door is left open to allow built-up smoke to escape and to cool the air just a bit. A snow rub-down or quick dip through a hole in the ice serves as a bracing way to cool off.

THE CASE FOR BLACK OR WHITE

Aalto called the old-fashioned smoke sauna "the sweeter sauna" and designed one for himself. It is appealing for its plain not-quite-square form and for the pitch-blackness of its interior. The only decoration is a checkered curtain at each of the two windows. The log hut, with its gently sloped roof, is an easy walk to the sea. Here Aalto swam for exercise, measuring his course between stalks of sea grass.

In contrast, is an unconventional white sauna that is large and comfortable enough to weekend in if one chooses. To its architect Hans Slangus, the whiteness stands for the purification of mind and body that are part of the bathing experience. The goal is to bear one's soul as well as body, to sit without pretense in sauna.

In the *savusauna*, a linen towel is laid on the bench to protect bathers from soot collected during the hours of smoky heating.

The bathing room, with three tiers of benches, seats several with ease and gives direct access to the sea without passing through the outer room. A grill there is used to cook after-sauna sausages, accompanied by beer.

Sauna gear is simple, beautiful and functional. Wood is traditionally used for the interior, as it is for fittings, since it remains relatively cool to the touch when temperatures rise. A slatted wood mat may be used on the floor and removed to dry out; a slatted headrest is preferred by those who like to recline in the sauna. Buckets, though also available in steel or plastic, are usually of wood and come in all sizes. They are used both for rinsing off after bathing—each person mixes hot and cold water to his taste—and for ladling water onto the hot rocks to create steam. Linen towels and washcloths range from soft homespuns to rougher looped weaves for an invigorating rub.

Different kinds of root brushes and loofahs are for cleansing bathers' backs; other brushes are for washing down benches after use. Non-polluting pine soaps are used for bathing in the lake or sea. Small flasks of birch essence are available as scent when fresh birch *vihtas* cannot be had.

ROUGH AND SMOOTH

A red farm sauna stands at the end of a lane. Its exterior sets the tone for an interior with homemade accessories: rag rugs that criss-cross its outer room, plaid curtains and striped terry towels.

The oldest and most primitive sauna huts were quickly and crudely assembled with uneven, untrimmed overlapping corners. The one at right was recently built in such fashion from freshly cut pines. Boards are laid down as walkways across its earth floor; rocks are piled loosely without mortar in a post-and-lintel arrangement to form the stove. The rooftop chimney is set high enough to clear snow accumulation, which provides insulation in winter weather. Other roof materials used, historically, were birchbark held in place with lengths of pine, peat moss or sod.

Red pine walls warm to textiles of the same tones.

Pines were crudely cut to build this sauna in a day; seams and corner joints are filled with moss. The door is made from young, slender trees and birchbark.

223

3
ELEMENTS

THE ELEMENTS

Finland is a country where the industrial age dawned on both the neo-classical townhouse and the rural chimneyless hut. In the last half of the nineteenth century the revolution in how people worked began to radically change the way they lived—nearly a century later than in southern Europe and America. In a very real sense, industrial design encountered primitive handicraft, a meeting that was to be influential in the years to follow.

Still in use in remote areas, the chimneyless log cabin that originated in medieval times in this dark northern country would hardly seem a logical link in the chain of important design for home interiors. What natural light existed entered through one small, shuttered opening and a ceiling vent used to draw out the smoke, and fell on walls blackened by years of cooking and heating fires laid in a stone hearth without a flue. Firelight and burning wood shingles or wax tapers otherwise illuminated the space. In the dim and sometimes smoky room, low priority was given to the decoration of furnishings; yet here were conceived the simple but beautifully proportioned long tables and benches, woven textiles and embroideries, tools and sleds that were to serve as models for clean design later and are prized today in their own right. The freestanding chair had become the first significant piece of furniture, a place of honor for the master of the house or a special guest. The importance of home, not just as shelter from the demanding climate, but as workroom for crafted objects, was established and has endured through the centuries.

With the coming of industrialization and the subsequent population pull toward cities, the medieval guild system that had fostered good workmanship among far-flung craftsmen declined. But in its place, those concerned with the continuity of esthetic traditions founded the School of Applied Arts in 1871 and, shortly after, the Society of Crafts and Design, and the Friends of Finnish Handicraft. It is largely through the efforts of these organizations, dedicated to the dissemination of information, conservation of objects and teaching of technique, that an important connection was established between crafts and industry at the time when factories were being established. The transition from handwork to work produced by the hands of many was facilitated. Industrialists became persuaded that good design meant substantial production and sales. Large ateliers were set up by the leading companies in glass and ceramics, and later in textiles and furniture, to provide on-staff artists with the materials and opportunity to create. Such provisions bore fruit first within the country in filling needs for new housing and domestic articles, and afterwards in prestigious design fairs in Stockholm, Paris, New York and Milan. International judges recognized the fine fabrication and fresh design.

One of the critical factors in the success of Finnish design in modern times was the emergence of the functionalist esthetic as a design solution in the early days of the young republic. Finland achieved nationhood in 1917. In the years immediately following, the Bauhaus was formulating a function-related philosophy proposing the integration of straightforward forms and industrially produced materials to fashion a new harmonious environment. These ideas found an appreciative audience among Finland's avant-garde and soon found a place in serious design schemes for state buildings and town planning. Functionalism—a justification of good design as useful—appealed to practical Finns on the most basic level and was adopted as a progressive badge of national identity. Further, Finland learned to develop and market modern products and systems to build the economy, and eventually to repay war reparations in full.

Much has been written on the virtues of contemporary Finnish design and craft. A brief description of some of their qualities and a sampling of objects from all categories representative of Finnish skills follow. Although an attempt has been made to cover important postwar designers, the task has been made difficult by the vast range of good work. Availability of articles has influenced those choices; certain categories where the Finnish contribution is highly regarded have not been included simply due to space limitations—for example, art textiles and glass, children's furniture and toys, and such. Further, many items not seen here will be found in the interiors on the preceding pages.

The design of objects in Finland is viewed as part of the overall social context. It is living design in the broadest sense—from ice breakers to coffee pots, toys to mailboxes, and buckets to chairs, design decisions are taken with deliberation and in earnest. Goals are both lofty and down-to-earth—availability, affordability, usefulness and beauty. Finns have achieved the production of what Swedish design critic, Ulf Hård af Segerstad, refers to as "the first-rate everyday object." Things, both buildings and their contents, are drawn and articulated in human scale. Design is for man, and man is part of nature; the connection is immediate, at once logical and romantic. Finnish design is sensual, it invites the human touch. An appreciation for materials has developed a talent for working with them to enhance their appeal. Object design shows care, the result of patience in fabricating a solution—a tendency handed down by craftsmen used to working in solitude with few precious resources available. There is a commitment to a lasting esthetic, a distaste for wastefulness and flash-in-the-pan trends. Much of the glassware and furniture originally created in the 1930's and 1940's and even earlier is still valid, and still in production. Lastly, this is quiet design, demonstrating more regard for harmony than showmanship. Like the Finns as a people, it shows strength, endurance and reserve.

Ateljee chair by Yrjö Kukkapuro for Avarte; steel and birch with leather, 1964.

A production process designed to be energy efficient and a unique pin suspension system for joining molded parts distinguish these chairs and coordinating table and desk collection. *Vivero* series by Yrjö Wiherheimo and Simo Heikkilä for Economic Kaluste; components of birch plywood and enameled steel, wool upholstery fabric by Irma Kukkasjärvi, 1979-80.

Clockwise: Module cabinet system by Pirkko Stenros for Muurame, birch, 1955; fan-leg tables by Alvar Aalto for Artek, birch with ash veneer, 1954; *Paimio* chair by Alvar Aalto for Artek, birch plywood, 1931; garden bench by Antti Nurmesniemi for Vuokko, plastic-coated steel with cotton covers, 1983.

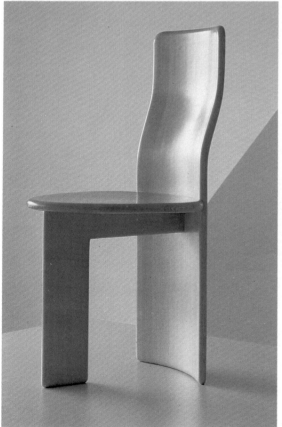

On this page, old and new designs, clockwise: chairs and table by Jouko Jarvisalo for Domeco, birch, 1982; platter by Timo Sarpaneva for Opa, polished and brushed steel, 1971; folding screen by Alvar Aalto for Artek, birch, mid-1930s; in the distance, *Finessi* chair by Matti Manner, enameled steel tube with leather cover, 1983; *Kukka* dish by Alvar Aalto for Iittala, opal glass, 1938; chair by Antti Nurmesniemi for Vuokko, Oregon pine, 1983.

On the opposite page, are some of the new, slim furniture silhouettes introduced within the last two years. Foreground to rear: experimental chair by Simo Heikkilä, enameled steel tube and birch plywood with wool upholstery, 1982; chair 115 by Harri Korhonen for Inno, enameled steel tube and birch plywood, 1983; *Experiments* chairs by Yrjö Kukkapuro for Avarte, steel tube and birch plywood with leather covers, 1982; *Inna* chair by Pentti Hakala for Inno, steel tube and birch plywood with woven linen cover by Irma Kukkasjärvi, 1982.

The art of glassmaking in Finland is three hundred years old and includes an array of high quality, hand-blown pieces, some shown here, as well as those that are serially produced. Clockwise: goblets and vase by Saara Hopea for Arabia/Nuutajärvi, 1957; 18th-century "forest glass" in amber and green tones; filigree bottle and graal bowls by Heikki Orvola for Arabia/Nuutajärvi, 1981; beakers by Kaj Franck for Arabia/Nuutajärvi, 1954.

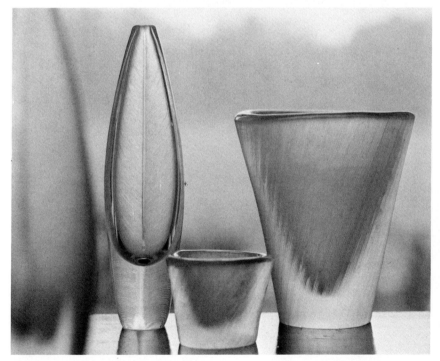

On this page, clockwise: filigree bottle by Heikki Orvola for Arabia/Nuuta-järvi, 1982; pressed glass goblets in traditional shape by Arabia/Nuutajärvi for Marimekko; vases by Tapio Wirkkala for Iittala, 1955; range of vases and bowls by Tapio Wirkkala for Iittala, 1951.

Country crafts, as they were and as they are made today, are shown here. Top, farm-made, 18th-century pieces: kitchen bowl carved from a single piece of wood; woven root basket; tin candlesticks and covered box; sour-milk container with oxblood stain, taken into the fields by farm hands. Bottom, pieces from this century made by traditional hand methods: woven birchbark baskets, heavy linen towel, cheese mold, aspen lidded butter box, juniper knives, fir spoon, birch tree-round carving boards.

Strong, simple shapes made by modern glass-blowing techniques and ceramics hand-thrown by potters in small studios are grouped here. Top: *Jurmo* vases by Timo Sarpaneva for Iittala, opal glass, 1979; vase and bowl by Sinikka Ahla, clay, 1983; late-18th-century pine table and upholstered chair made for the town hall at Rauma. Bottom: *Iris* pottery by A. W. Finch, 1897-1902; 18th-century pine table and chairs, and linen runner.

Some of the modern inheritors of the centuries-old textile tradition are assembled on this page. Clockwise: printed cotton by Anneli Airikka-Lammi for Tampella, 1983; printed cotton by Vuokko, 1983; woven cotton by Laila Leppänen and Kaarina Berglund for Finlayson, 1983; woven cotton in *poppana* technique by Annikki Karvinen, early 1980s.

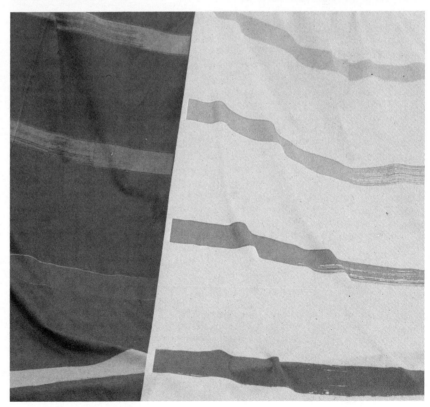

Clockwise: cotton terry by Markku Piri for Finlayson, 1983; printed cotton by Alvar Aalto for Artek, 1954; printed cotton by Fujiwo Ishimoto for Marimekko, 1981; wool blanket by Marimekko, early 1980s; wool weaving in *raanu* and *ryijy* techniques by Kirsti Rantanen, 1970s; cotton string blanket by Salme Karvanen, 1983.

A few handmade pieces from the independent studios now supporting a substantial number of artist-craftspeople: bowl on tripod by Heikki Kallio, glass and wood with leather thong; footed pots and perfume bottle with iridescent glaze by Åsa Hellman, ceramic; vase by Hilkka Jarva, ceramic—all are made in the early 1980s.

The continued use of light, natural wood takes many divergent forms. This page, clockwise: split-wood baskets from the marketplace; *Kari 1* chair and table by Kari Asikainen for Korhonen, birch with raffia cover, 1969; root brushes from the marketplace; country-style chairs from various manufacturers, pine.

Kitchen utensils of wood from the marketplace; traditional seed basket for sowing grain; traditional woven birchbark basket; platter by Saarinen, birch plywood, late 1970s; *Gardenside* sofa by Avitom, pine with linen and cotton covers by Metsovaara, 1960.

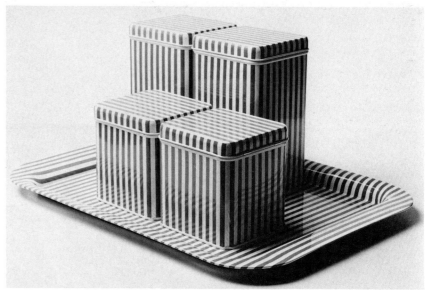

This page, clockwise; coffeepot by Antti Nurmesniemi for Arabia, enameled steel, 1958; painted tin boxes by Marimekko, late 1970s; basket by Kotikäsityö, birchbark; *Kokki* cookware by Tapio Yli-Viikari for Arabia, flameproof ceramic, 1977; mortar and pestle, cup and covered bowl by Jukka Tommila, Karelian soapstone, early 1980s.

Opposite, clockwise: Gyro chair by Eero Aarnio for Asko, fiberglass, 1968; covered butter dish and knife by Karin Weckström, 1980; *puukko* knife by Tapio Wirkkala for Hackman, stainless steel and brass with leather case, 1963; flasks by Opa, polished steel, early 1980s; traditional bowls, clay; oven mitts by Vuokko, cotton, late 1970s.

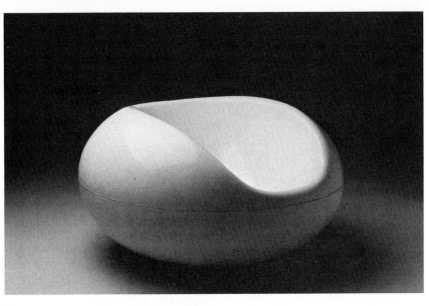

This page, clockwise: lamps by Jouko Kuha for Marimekko, enameled aluminum, mid-1970s; wooden ladle and kitchen utensil for blending food or hanging gear, from marketplace; bowl by Martti Kyppänen for Artek, curly birch, early 1980s; candlesticks by Bertel Gardberg, pewter with brass lining, 1950s; *Easy Day* dishes and cutlery by Kaj Franck for Sarvis, 1978.

Opposite, clockwise: *Kilta* stackable dishes and serving pieces by Kaj Franck for Arabia, stoneware, 1952 and 1981; platters and bowls by Terhi Juurinen and Riita Pensanen for Seenat, ceramic, 1977; *Aarne* glasses by Göran Hongell for Iittala, 1948; *Kari 3* chair by Kari Asikainen for Korhonen, birch, 1982; scissors range by Olof Bäckström and Olavi Lindén for Fiskars, 1963; lamp by Yki Nummi for Stockman Orno, acrylic, 1955.

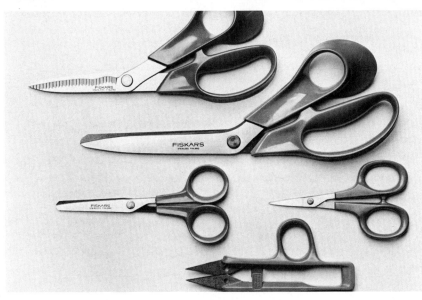

SOURCES/ UNITED STATES

Ad Hoc Softwares
410 West Broadway
New York, New York 10012
linens

Barry Friedman Ltd.
26 East 82nd Street
New York, New York 10028
early modern furniture

Beylerian Ltd.
305 East 63rd Street
New York, New York 10021
furniture by Kukkapuro

Conrans
160 East 54th Street
New York, New York 10022
textiles, home furnishings

Crate and Barrel
850 N. Michigan Avenue
Chicago, Illinois 60611
textiles, home furnishings

Crate and Barrel
Faneuil Hall Marketplace
Boston, Massachusetts 02109
textiles, home furnishings

Evergreen Antiques
120 Spring Street
New York, New York 10012
antique pine, rag rugs

Fabrications
146 East 56th Street
New York, New York 10022
textiles

Fifty/50
793 Broadway
New York, New York 10003
early modern glass, furniture

Finlandia Furniture
1827 Newport Boulevard
Costa Mesa, California 92627
furniture

ICF
305 East 63rd Street
New York, New York 10021
furniture by Aalto, Saarinen

ICF
8687 Melrose Avenue
Los Angeles, California 90069
furniture by Aalto, Saarinen

Luminaire
2331 Ponce De Leon Boulevard
Coral Gables, Florida 33134
furniture, textiles

Marimekko
7 West 56th Street
New York, New York 10019
textiles, home furnishings

Marimekko
50 Post Street
San Francisco, California 94104
textiles, home furnishings

Marimekko
8939 Metcalf
Overland Park, Kansas 66212
textiles, home furnishings

Modernism
984 Madison Avenue
New York, New York 10021
early modern furniture

Museum of Modern Art Gift Shop
11 West 53rd Street
New York, New York 10019
furniture by Aalto, accessories

Scan
3222 M Street, Georgetown
Washington, D.C. 20007
furniture

Scan
1407 York Road
Lutherville, Maryland 21093
furniture

Scandinavian Design
127 East 59th Street
New York, New York 10022
furniture

Sointu Design
20 East 69th Street
New York, New York 10021
glass, accessories

D. F. Sanders & Co.
386 West Broadway
New York, New York 10012
furniture, accessories

Whiteley Galleries
111 N. La Brea Avenue
Los Angeles, California 90036
early modern furniture

Workbench
470 Park Avenue South
New York, New York 10016
furniture

SOURCES/ FINLAND

Aarikka
Pohjoisesplanadi 25-27
00100 Helsinki 10
woodenware

Annikki Karvinen
Unioninkatu 30
00100 Helsinki 10
textiles, woven fittings

Arabia/Nuutajärvi
Pohjoisesplanadi 25
00100 Helsinki 10
ceramics, glass, cookware

Art Forge/Konstsmide
Fabianinkatu 4
00130 Helsinki 13
soapstone articles, metalwork

Artek
Keskuskatu 3
10100 Helsinki 10
furniture, home furnishings

Artisaani
Unioninkatu 28
00100 Helsinki 10
crafts

Avarte
Telakkakatu 3
00150 Helsinki 15
furniture by Kukkapuro

Catalina
Kasarmikatu 19
00130 Helsinki 13
rag rugs

Decembre
Pietarinkatu 10
00140 Helsinki 14
accessories, furniture

Economic-Kaluste
Kiviaidankatu 11
00210 Helsinki 21
furniture by Heikkilä, Wiherheimo

Finnish Design Center
Kasarmikatu 19
00130 Helsinki 13
home furnishings, crafts

Friends of Finnish Handicraft
Meilahti 7
00250 Helsinki 25
textiles, crafts, rya rugs

Hopea
Mannerheiminkatu 12
06100 Porvoo
silver, glass

I-Shop
Pohjoisesplanadi 27
00100 Helsinki 10
glass, cutlery

Indoor
Fabianinkatu 14
00100 Helsinki 10
furniture, home furnishings

Inno
Pietarinkatu 9
00140 Helsinki 14
furniture, lighting

Korhonen
Maariankatu 3b
20100 Turku 10
furniture, home furnishings

Lauri-Tuotteet
Pohjolankatu 25
96100 Rovaniemi 10
woodenware, cutlery

Marimekko
Pohjoisesplanadi 31
00100 Helsinki 10
textiles, home furnishings

Marja Harmes
Fredrikinkatu 24
00120 Helsinki 12
rag rugs

Pentik
Pohjoisesplanadi 25A
00100 Helsinki 10
ceramics, woodenware

Pirta
Museokatu 15
00100 Helsinki 10
rag rugs

Pot Viapori
Island of Suomenlinna
00190 Helsinki 19
crafts studios, shops

Sauna Shop
Mannerheimintie 22-24
00100 Helsinki 10
wooden articles, linens

Stockmann Department Store
Aleksanterinkatu 52
Helsinki
furniture, home furnishings

Vuokko
Fabiankatu 12
00100 Helsinki 10
textiles

Vuokko
Merikatu 1
00140 Helsinki 14
textiles, furniture

MUSEUMS/
UNITED STATES

Cooper-Hewitt Museum
2 East 91st Street
New York, New York 10028

Corning Museum of Glass
Corning Glass Center
Museum Way
Corning, New York 14831

Cranbrook Academy of Art Museum
500 Lone Pine Road
Bloomfield Hills, Michigan 48013

Metropolitan Museum of Art
Fifth Avenue and 82nd Street
New York, New York 10028

Museum of Decorative Arts
2929 Jeanne D'Arc
Montreal, Canada

Museum of Modern Art
11 West 53rd Street
New York, New York 10019

Museum of Modern Art
Van Ness and McAllister
San Francisco, California

Philadelphia Museum of Art
26 Benjamin Franklin Parkway
Philadelphia, Pennsylvania 19103

MUSEUMS/
FINLAND

Gallen-Kallela Museum and House
Gallen-Kallelantie 27
02600 Espoo 60

Helsinki City Museum
Karamzininkatu 2
00100 Helsinki 10

Hvitträsk
Eliel Saarinen House
12440 Luomi, Kirkkonummi

Iittala Glassworks
14500 Iittala

Kirsti Museum
Pohjankatu 3
26100 Rauma

Museum of Applied Arts
Korkeavuorenkatu 23
00130 Helsinki 13

Museum of Finnish Architecture
Kasarmikatu 24
00130 Helsinki 13

National Museum of Finland
Mannerheimintie 34
00100 Helsinki 10

Sauna Museum
40950 Muurame

Seurasaari Open-Air Museum
Island of Seurasaari
00250 Helsinki 25

Villa Mairea
Alvar Aalto Architecture, Interiors
Noormarkku
July, August only

Nuutajärvi Glassworks
31160 Nuutajärvi

Porvoo Museum
Välikatu 11
06100 Porvoo

Rauma Museum
Kauppakatu 13
26100 Rauma

Riihimäki Glass Museum
Tehtaankatu 23
11100 Riihimäki

SELECTED BIBLIOGRAPHY

Abacus 3. Edited by Asko Salokorpi and Maija Karrainen. Helsinki: Museum of Finnish Architecture, 1983.

Alvar Aalto and the International Style. Paul David Pearson. New York: Whitney Library of Design, 1978.

Eight-Hundred Years of Finnish Architecture. J. M. Richards. London: David & Charles, 1978.

Eliel Saarinen. Albert W. Christ-Janer. Chicago: University of Chicago Press, 1948.

Finland Creates. Jack Fields and David Moore. Jyväskyla: Gummerus, 1977.

Finland, Land of the Midnight Sun. Oy Valitut Palat. Helsinki: Reader's Digest Ab, 1978.

Finland: Nature, Design, Architecture. Finnish Society of Crafts and Design, and Museum of Finnish Architecture. Helsinki: 1981.

Finland, the New Nation. Agnes Rothery. New York: Viking Press, 1937.

Finnish Architecture. Nils Erik Wickberg. Helsinki: Otava, 1959.

Finnish Design 1875-1975. Finnish Society of Crafts and Design. Helsinki: Otava, 1975.

Finnish Reflections. Kalervo Siikala. Helsinki: Kirjayhtyma, 1981.

Helsinki Architectural Guide. Helsinki: Otava, 1976.

Modern Finnish Design. Ulf Hård af Segerstad. New York: Praeger, 1969.

Of Finnish Ways. Aini Rajanen. Minneapolis: Dillon Press, 1981.

Ornamo Book. Ornamo and Finnish Society of Crafts and Design. Edited by Armi Ratia. Helsinki: 1962.

Sauna. A. Reinikainen. Helsinki: MTR-Studio, 1977.

Scandinavian Design. Edited by David McFadden. New York: Harry Abrams, 1982.

Siren. Heikki and Kaija Siren. Helsinki: Otava, 1977.

The Things Around Us. Finnish Society of Crafts and Design. Helsinki: Otava, 1981.

CREDITS

photographs on pages 36–43 courtesy of *House & Garden*
photographs of reindeer, p. 175 Bo Niles
quote from Agnes Rothery, p. 183 *Finland, the New Nation* (New York: Viking Press, 1937).